Primitive Style
Folk-Art Quilts and Other Finery

JENIFER GASTON

Martingale®
Create with Confidence

Primitive Style: Folk-Art Quilts and Other Finery
© 2015 by Jenifer Gaston

Martingale®
19021 120th Ave. NE, Ste. 102
Bothell, WA 98011-9511 USA
ShopMartingale.com

Printed in China
20 19 18 17 16 15   8 7 6 5 4 3 2 1

Library of Congress Cataloging-in-Publication Data is available upon request.

ISBN: 978-1-60468-683-8

MISSION STATEMENT
Dedicated to providing quality products and service to inspire creativity.

CREDITS
PUBLISHER AND CHIEF VISIONARY OFFICER
Jennifer Erbe Keltner

EDITORIAL DIRECTOR
Karen Costello Soltys

DESIGN DIRECTOR
Paula Schlosser

MANAGING EDITOR
Tina Cook

PHOTOGRAPHER
Brent Kane

ACQUISITIONS EDITOR
Karen M. Burns

PRODUCTION MANAGER
Regina Girard

TECHNICAL EDITOR
Ellen Pahl

INTERIOR DESIGNER
Adrienne Smitke

COPY EDITOR
Melissa Bryan

ILLUSTRATOR
Anne Moscicki

Thanks to Rosemary and Cliff Bailey of Snohomish, Washington, for allowing the photography for this book to take place in their home.

Contents

An Introduction to Primitive Style

What is "primitive style"? To me, it's an easy, casual style. I like to think of the pioneer woman making things for her home with the materials she could find or that she had on hand. She would appliqué flowers, animals, or everyday objects on her quilts, or hook them in her rugs. The designs were simple and full of character—in other words, primitive—because she wouldn't have been a trained artist.

While making useful and essential items for the home, she was conveying a bit about the story of her life through the images and designs she chose to incorporate. She also would have used her projects as a way to be creative and show her personality. A house might be smaller than the flowers around it. The cat might be larger than the tree. You might even find a person with purple skin on a primitive quilt!

The quilting on these items might not consist of the tiniest stitches or the most intricate designs, because she would need to get that quilt on a bed quickly to keep a loved one warm. But her quilts and rugs would be very well made to stand the test of time, so that she wouldn't have to keep mending them often. When she did have to mend them, she would patch them up with love.

I do know that a woman was considered a "good catch" if she could sew and embroider well, so "primitive" doesn't mean that an item isn't well made, or that it wasn't well made when it was new 200 years ago!

I believe that most of us who love the primitive style are drawn to relatively dark, soft colors because they are easy on the eyes and project a cozy feeling. But I think you can just as easily make a beautiful primitive-style quilt in bright colors or modern prints if you like. I would bet that those pioneer women would have loved to find something bright and colorful to cheer up their homes if they could have!

I often think of my great-grandmother. If she'd had a rotary cutter, mat, and long-arm quilting machine, she would have used them and made *a lot* more quilts! So I don't think you have to be a purist to make projects in the primitive style. While I love how my modern tools help make quiltmaking easier in many ways, I also love the slow, calming process of handwork that allows you to imagine the days of old.

If you want your primitive-style project to look old using your new fabrics, try one of these techniques.

- Dye your fabrics with tan dye or a concentrated mixture of instant coffee. I often dye the entire finished quilt with coffee or tan Rit dye.

- If you have any fabrics that are a bit brighter than you'd like, dye them before using them in a quilt or other project. I always dye osnaburg before using it, whether the other fabrics are dyed or not. Osnaburg is a coarsely woven cotton fabric commonly used for crafts and primitive-style projects.

- Rough up spots on the fabric with sandpaper.

- Stitch on little patches here and there to suggest the wear and tear of a well-loved vintage item.

- Use several types of fabric in one project, relying only on what you have on hand, to add texture and give your project an authentic "make do" feeling.

I recommend simply doing what you like to give your primitive-style project the character and feel you're looking for. Don't be afraid—just play, and prepare to be pleasantly surprised by the results!

~ Jenifer

Close at Hand

I love to have a handmade pincushion nearby, always ready when I need it. In my opinion, you can never have enough! I keep one by my sewing machines, one near my favorite chair for hand sewing, and one on my dresser to hold safety pins. Pincushions also make great gifts for your sewing pals, so why not make a few?

FINISHED PINCUSHION 6" x 8"

Materials

All wool is hand dyed; piece sizes are based on wool that has been felted and is ready to use.

7" x 9" piece of army-green wool for pincushion bottom
5" x 7" piece of brown-plaid wool for pincushion top
4" x 6" piece of tan wool for hand
1½" x 2½" piece of red wool for heart
1 fat eighth (9" x 21") of muslin for lining
Wool thread in dark brown, red, tan, and light brown
16 ounces of crushed walnut shells for stuffing
Chalk wheel or chalk pencil
Small, sharp scissors
Funnel

Cutting

From the brown-plaid wool, cut:
1 rectangle, 4½" x 6½"

From the army-green wool, cut:
1 rectangle, 6½" x 8½"

From the muslin, cut:
1 rectangle, 6½" x 9"

Making the Pincushion

1. Referring to "Wool Appliqué" on page 70, cut out the appliqué shapes using the patterns for the hand and heart on pullout pattern sheet 1.

2. Center the heart and hand on the brown-plaid wool 4½" x 6½" rectangle and pin in place or tack with fabric glue. The hand should overlap the lower portion of the heart by about ⅛". Whipstitch both pieces with matching wool thread.

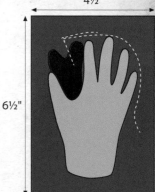

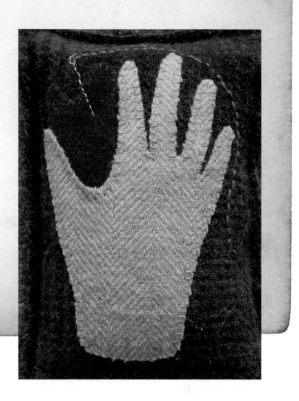

appliquéd piece using dark-brown wool thread and a backstitch. Leave one short side open.

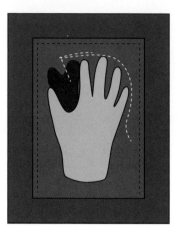

3. With a chalk wheel or chalk pencil, draw the needle and thread onto the heart and brown-wool background. You can do this freehand, or refer to "Tracing Designs onto Wool" below. Stitch the needle with a backstitch using tan wool thread. Stitch the thread line with a backstitch using one strand of red and one strand of light-brown wool thread together.

5. Make a bag for the walnut shells by folding the muslin rectangle in half to measure 4½" x 6½". Sew by machine all the way around with a ¼" seam allowance, leaving a 2" opening.

6. Turn the bag right side out, and use a funnel to fill with the walnut shells. Stitch the opening closed by hand.

7. Insert the bag into the stitched piece and sew the last side closed using a backstitch.

8. Using very sharp, small scissors, hand cut a zigzag edge in the green-wool backing, purposely not trying to make each cut perfect. That's my secret for your project turning out successfully—perfection isn't required!

Tracing Designs onto Wool

Place a piece of nylon netting over the paper pattern and tape it in place. Use a Sharpie marker to trace the images onto the netting. Pin the marked netting on the wool and trace over the design with a chalk wheel or chalk pencil. Remove the netting, and you'll see the lines drawn on the wool.

4. With the wrong side down, position the appliquéd piece in the center of the army-green wool 6½" x 8½" rectangle. Pin in place and stitch ¼" from three raw edges of the

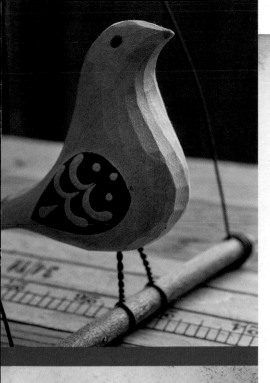

Cozy Home

Materials

All wool is hand dyed; piece sizes are based on wool that has been felted and is ready to use.

⅜ yard of solid-red homespun fabric for cover
¼ yard of osnaburg fabric for appliqué background
4" x 4" piece of blue wool for house
2" x 4" piece of brown-plaid wool for roof
2½" x 2½" piece of brown wool for windows
1½" x 3" piece of black wool for crow
1" x 2" piece of black-and-tan wool for wing
1" x 1½" piece of red wool for door
10½" x 15½" piece of thin cotton batting
Wool thread in colors to match appliqués
Black quilting thread
Composition notebook

Cutting

From the red homespun, cut:
1 strip, 10½" x 42"; cut in half to make 2 strips, 10½" x 21"

From the osnaburg, cut *on the lengthwise grain:*
1 rectangle, 5¼" x 7½"

> ### On the Fringe
>
> To fray the osnaburg fabric, use a pin to pull the threads at the edges. Gently pull them out evenly on all four sides, leaving a fringe at a length that you like. You may need to trim the fringe with sharp scissors if the fabric wasn't cut on the straight of grain.

*J*ust as I can never have too many pincushions, I never seem to have enough notebooks! I use them for making lists and for taking notes in meetings. I also doodle in them to come up with new quilting designs and rug-hooking patterns. Why not make a fun notebook cover for yourself, and some for your pals!

FINISHED COVER
7½" x 9¾" (fits a standard composition notebook)

Making the Journal Cover

1. Fold the cut ends of the red homespun strips (the 10½" ends without selvage) to the wrong side ¼" and press. Fold ¼" again and press. Stitch by machine close to the inner folded edges to make a hem.

2. Lay the two red pieces right sides together and place the batting on top, centering it on the homespun. Pin in place and sew both long sides using a ¼" seam allowance. Turn right side out and press.

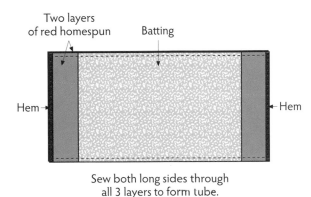

Sew both long sides through
all 3 layers to form tube.

3. Fold back the front and back covers of the notebook and insert them into the open ends of the cover approximately 3". Close the notebook. Adjust the cover to make it fit as snugly as possible. Be sure that the flaps on the front and back covers are the same dimension (if it's 3" wide on the front, it should be 3" wide on the back).

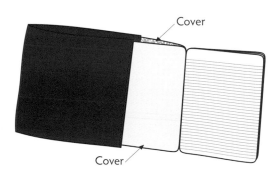

4. Referring to "Wool Appliqué" on page 70, cut out the appliqué shapes using the patterns on pullout pattern sheet 1.

5. Fray the edges of the osnaburg 5¼" x 7½" rectangle about ¼" on all four sides. (See "On the Fringe" on page 9.)

6. Arrange the wool pieces on the osnaburg; pin, and stitch in place with matching threads.

7. Center the stitched piece on the front of the journal cover. Pin in place and remove the cover from the notebook.

8. With black quilting thread, sew a running stitch around the osnaburg ½" from the frayed edges to secure the fabric to the journal cover.

9. Insert the notebook back into the cover. Use a small whipstitch and matching thread to sew the top and bottom edges of the notebook cover to the flaps, making sure the fit is nice and snug.

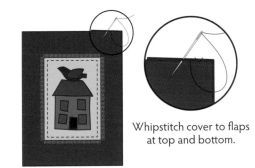

Whipstitch cover to flaps
at top and bottom.

Woolly Bird

Stitch a cute appliquéd wool sewing pouch that's quick to make and just the thing to hold your current hand-stitching project and supplies. The vinyl window allows you to see at a glance if everything is there. The pouch can fit in your tote bag or purse, ready to go at a moment's notice!

FINISHED POUCH
9" x 10"

Materials

All wool is hand dyed; piece sizes are based on wool that has been felted and is ready to use. Vinyl comes on 60"-wide rolls.

1 fat quarter (18" x 21") of cotton print for lining
8" x 16" piece of red wool for pouch front
8" x 10" piece of olive-green wool for pouch back
5" x 10" piece of beige-plaid wool for pouch back
4" x 7" piece of black wool for birds
2" x 3½" piece of red-plaid wool for large bird wing
1½" x 1½" piece of blue-plaid wool for flower
1" x 1½" piece of gray wool for small bird wing
1" x 1" piece of orange wool for flower center
¼ yard of vinyl for window
9" black zipper
⅓ yard of 20"-wide fusible web
Wool thread in colors to match appliqués
Size 8 pearl cotton in black, khaki, cream, and green
Tissue paper (optional)

Cutting

From the red wool, cut:
2 rectangles, 3" x 9½"
2 rectangles, 1½" x 5½"

From the olive-green wool, cut:
1 rectangle, 7" x 9½"

From the vinyl, cut:
1 rectangle, 5½" x 7½"

From the beige-plaid wool, cut:
1 rectangle, 4" x 9½"

From the cotton print, cut:
1 rectangle, 9½" x 10½"

From the fusible web, cut:
1 rectangle, 9¼" x 10¼"

Appliquéing the Pouch Pieces

1. Referring to "Wool Appliqué" on page 70, cut out the appliqué shapes using the patterns for the birds and flower on pullout pattern sheet 1.

2. Appliqué the small bird and wing in the center of one red-wool 3" x 9½" rectangle using a whipstitch. Use the green pearl cotton to feather stitch across the bottom for the bird's branch, and make French knots at the tip of each "feather" with the khaki pearl cotton. Add a French knot for the bird's eye. Refer to "Embroidery Stitches" on page 71 for details.

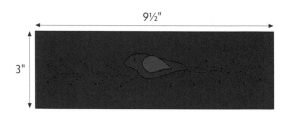

3. Center the large bird on the olive-green wool 7" x 9½" rectangle, and appliqué it with a running stitch ¼" from the raw edge of the wool shape. Stitch the wing to the bird in the same manner.

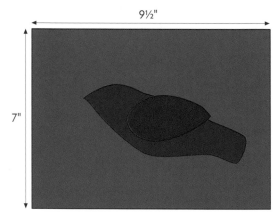

4. Appliqué the orange circle to the blue-plaid flower with four long stitches across the center. Tack stitch at the center and add a French knot.

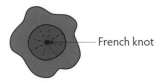
French knot

5. Embroider the bird's feet with black pearl cotton and the flower stem with khaki pearl cotton using a backstitch. Make lazy daisy stitches for the leaves with khaki pearl cotton, referring to "Embroidery Stitches."

6. Appliqué the flower unit to the top of the stem using a whipstitch.

Assembling the Pouch

Use a ¼" seam allowance for all steps.

1. Sew the red-wool 1½" x 5½" rectangles to opposite sides of the vinyl 5½" x 7½" rectangle.

Easy Sewing

Place a piece of tissue paper between the vinyl and your machine so that the layers will glide easily. When you're done sewing, simply tear off the tissue paper.

2. Sew the appliquéd red-wool rectangle to the bottom edge of the vinyl and the remaining red-wool 3" x 9½" rectangle to the top.

3. Topstitch on the wool around the window to keep the seams nice and flat.

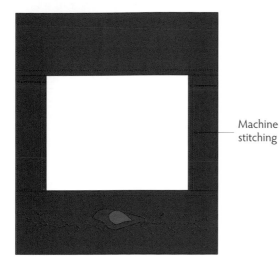

Machine stitching

4. Stitch the beige-plaid wool 4" x 9½" rectangle and the appliquéd olive-green wool rectangle together, positioning the appliquéd piece along what will be the bottom of the pouch. Press the seam allowances open and topstitch on both sides of the seam by hand using a running stitch. I used black thread on the cream wool and cream thread on the olive-green wool.

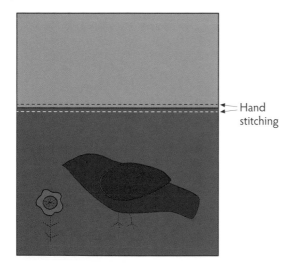

Hand stitching

5. Iron the fusible web to the wrong side of the cotton-print 9½" x 10½" rectangle for the lining. Allow to cool, and then remove the paper backing. Fuse the lining to the wrong side of the appliquéd pouch back from step 4 to cover up the seam allowances and threads.

6. With right sides together, sew one side of the zipper to the top of the pouch front, using a zipper foot if desired.

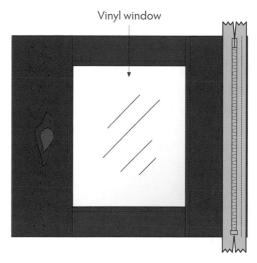

Vinyl window

Sew zipper to right side of bag front.

7. Repeat step 6 to sew the zipper to the back of the pouch. After sewing a few inches, stop with the needle down and lift the presser foot. Unzip the zipper partway and continue sewing the rest of the way down the zipper.

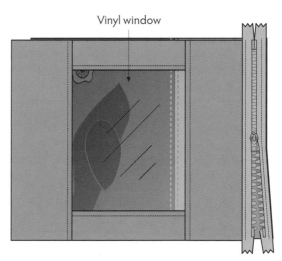

Vinyl window

Align bag front and back with right sides together and sew zipper to right side of bag back.

Just a couple simple embroidery stitches add so much charm to the final project!

8. Fold the piece with right sides together so that the zipper is at the top. With the zipper about halfway open, sew the three sides together, catching the ends of the zipper fabric. Backstitch at each end of the zipper for extra strength.

9. Turn the piece right side out, fill with your stitching necessities, and go!

Cotton print lining

Sew remaining three sides.

Sew and Hook

I love having something to corral all my tools for rug hooking and stitching. I can grab this roll, stick it in my bag, and go hung out with my sewing friends. Perfect for using up scraps, the appliquéd letters can be cut from bits and pieces left over from other projects.

FINISHED ROLL (flat)
12" x 25"

Materials

All wool is hand dyed; wool yardage and piece sizes are based on wool that has been felted and is ready to use.

½ yard of natural-color linen for exterior
⅜ yard of army-green wool for interior*
9" x 12" piece of dark-green wool for exterior stems and leaves
8" x 11" piece of plum wool for pocket and 1 flower
8" x 9" piece of off-white wool for interior letters
6" x 10" piece of red wool for 3 flowers and exterior letters
6" x 10" piece of blue wool for pocket flap and 5 flowers
5" x 10" piece of black wool for pincushion
6" x 8" piece of green wool for interior stems and leaves
2" x 7" piece of orange wool for 5 flowers
3½" x 4" piece of light-brown houndstooth wool for spool
2" x 2" piece of light-orange wool for 1 flower
2" x 2" piece of light-gray wool for 1 flower
1 yard of ½"-wide black rayon ribbon
2 buttons, ½" to 1" diameter, for pocket flap
Handful of wool roving or stuffing for pincushion
Wool thread in colors to match appliqués
Size 8 pearl cotton in khaki

*If you have an army blanket that you don't mind cutting up, you can use that for the interior of the roll.

Cutting

From the linen, cut:
1 rectangle, 13" x 26"

From the army-green wool, cut:
1 rectangle, 12" x 25"

From the black wool, cut:
1 rectangle, 4½" x 9"

From the plum wool, cut:
1 rectangle, 7½" x 8½"

From the blue wool, cut:
1 pocket flap (pattern on pullout sheet 1)

From the dark-green wool, cut:
2 bias strips, ½" x 19"
2 bias strips, ¼" x 4"

Appliquéing the Exterior

1. Referring to "Wool Appliqué" on page 70, cut out the appliqué shapes for the exterior of the roll using the patterns for the flowers, leaves, and the word *SEW* on pullout pattern sheet 1.

2. Position and tack the dark-green bias strips and appliqués onto the linen 13" x 26" rectangle with pins or a little fabric glue. Stitch with a whipstitch and matching wool threads.

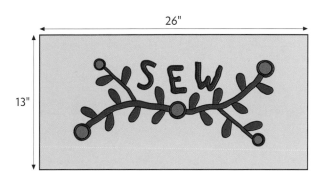

Appliquéing the Interior

1. Cut out the appliqué shapes for the interior of the roll using the patterns for the flowers, stems, leaves, spool, and the words *SNIP, HOOK,* and *PINS* on the pullout sheet.

2. Position and appliqué the words *SNIP* and *HOOK* to the plum-wool 7½" x 8½" rectangle as shown using a whipstitch. Allow about 2" along the left side for the pocket flaps and buttons.

3. Position and appliqué the word *PINS* on the black-wool 4½" x 9" rectangle using a whipstitch.

4. Using your buttons to determine length, cut buttonhole slits in the pocket flap. Whipstitch or blanket-stitch the raw edges of the buttonholes, and blanket-stitch the curved edges of the flap.

5. Blanket-stitch the left 7½" side of the plum pocket piece so that it will have a nice finish along the top.

6. Referring to the placement guide on page 20, place the plum pocket on the army-green 12" x 25" background. Place the flap underneath the pocket by about 1¾" and fold the flaps over. Whipstitch along the folded edge. Remove the plum pocket rectangle so that you can fold the flaps back and whipstitch all around the underneath portion of the flap. This will prevent tools from getting stuck under the flap when they are in the pocket.

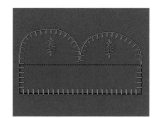

7. Replace the pocket and position the spool, stems, leaves, flowers, and the appliquéd pincushion piece from step 3 on the army-green background as shown. Stitch the appliqués using a whipstitch. Stitch a running stitch down the center of the pocket to create

Leave your tool roll flat and on display for easy access when at home. You can enjoy your handiwork on either side.

two compartments. As you stitch the pincushion, leave an opening and insert the wool roving or stuffing before completing the stitching.

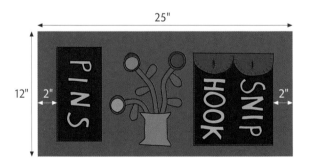

8. Sew the buttons to the pocket under the flap.

Finishing the Tool Roll

1. Fold the edges of the linen under ½" to the wrong side all the way around. Press and baste in place.

2. Place the linen wrong sides together with the army-green stitched piece. Pin together; baste if desired.

3. Cut a 30" length of ribbon and fold it in half. Pin it in place, centered on the edge next to the pockets. Whipstitch in place.

4. Using khaki pearl cotton, blanket-stitch the two layers together all the way around.

Blooms and Berries

Materials

All wool is hand dyed; piece sizes are based on wool that has been felted and is ready to use.

⅝ yard of osnaburg fabric for background*
6" x 6" piece of olive-green wool for flower stems and leaves
6" x 6" piece of red wool for berries and heart
6" x 6" piece of brown-plaid wool for berry stems and leaves
3" x 10" piece of blue-plaid wool for flowers
5" x 5" piece of brown wool for vase
2" x 6" piece of orange wool for flower centers
Wool thread in colors to match appliqués
Wooden frame with 14" x 14" opening

You can also use linen or another textured fabric for the background.

Cutting

From the osnaburg, cut:
1 square, 19" x 19"

From the olive-green wool, cut:
1 bias strip, ¼" x 7"
2 bias strips, ¼" x 6"
1 bias strip, ¼" x 4"

From the brown-plaid wool, cut:
2 bias strips, ¼" x 8"

Appliquéing the Background

1. Referring to "Wool Appliqué" on page 70, cut out the appliqué shapes using the patterns for the flowers, berries, heart, and vase on pullout pattern sheet 1. Cut leaves 3, 4, 11, 12, and 13 from the remainder of the brown-plaid wool. Cut the rest of the leaves from the remainder of the olive-green wool.

Framed to grace a wall in your home, or the home of a loved one, this wool appliqué piece is simple and quick to put together, and a wonderful way to make things instantly cozy! Wool scraps would find a happy home in this piece as well.

FINISHED APPLIQUÉ
14" x 14" without frame

2. Position the pieces on the osnaburg 19" background square as shown. Use pins or fabric glue to hold the pieces in place.

3. Whipstitch all of the pieces using matching threads.

4. Press from the wrong side with steam. Then turn right side up and press again using steam and a pressing cloth. Allow to dry flat.

Finishing the Piece

I had my piece framed professionally because premade frames with a 14" square opening aren't readily available. If you prefer to frame the piece yourself, you can purchase the supplies needed to make your own frame at a local craft shop. You'll also need a 14" square of cotton batting and a 14" square of mat board or cardboard.

1. Place the batting on the mat board and adhere it in place with glue or spray adhesive. Allow to dry.

2. Place the appliquéd piece on top of the batting, keeping the design centered. Fold the edges over to the back and tape in place using masking tape.

3. Insert into the frame.

Simple whipstitches and matching thread allow the pretty wools to get all of the attention!

Other Options

Here are some other suggestions for your wool appliquéd flowers and berries.

- Make a lovely square quilted table topper by layering with batting and backing. Quilt and add binding.

- Add a row of zigzag stitching ½" from all sides of the piece. Fray the edges to make a simple raw-edge scarf for a table or chest.

- Make a square pillow, trimming the piece to a smaller size if desired.

Resting Place

A sweet wool pillow will cozy up any sofa or chair. I love handwork, especially wool appliqué, and the tongues added on the sides of this pillow make it extra special. Make one for your favorite sewing chair and one for your favorite friend!

FINISHED PILLOW
22" x 12" (including tongues)

Materials

All wool is hand dyed; piece sizes are based on wool that has been felted and is ready to use.

25" x 30" piece of olive-green wool for branches, leaves, tongues, and pillow back*

13" x 17" piece of cream wool for pillow front

8" x 23" piece of dark-brown plaid wool for robin's body, wing, and tongues

6" x 10" piece of robin's egg–blue wool for flowers and penny circles

4" x 10" piece of light-pink houndstooth wool for flowers, robin's breast, and penny circles

Wool thread in colors to match appliqués

12" x 16" pillow form

*A thick coat-weight wool or an army blanket adds body to the pillow and tongues.

Cutting

Use the pattern for the tongues on pullout pattern sheet 2.

From the olive-green wool, cut:
2 rectangles, 10½" x 13"
8 tongues

From the dark-brown plaid, cut:
8 tongues

An Imperfect Look

To achieve a primitive style when cutting circles from wool, you can first cut several squares from the wool. Measure the diameter of the circle needed, and then cut squares to that size. Use scissors to round the corners to turn them into circles. They will be similar in size, but won't look too perfect!

Appliquéing the Pillow

1. Referring to "Wool Appliqué" on page 70, cut out the appliqué shapes using the patterns for the bird, branch, leaves, and flowers on pullout pattern sheet 2.

2. Position and pin or glue the appliqué pieces on the cream 13" x 17" background, using the pattern as a placement guide.

3. Whipstitch the pieces in place.

4. Cut out eight large penny circles from the blue wool and eight smaller penny circles from the pink wool using the patterns on the pullout sheet. Whipstitch the pink circles to the blue circles, and then appliqué them to the dark-brown plaid tongues using a whipstitch.

5. With wrong sides together, pin each plaid tongue to a green-wool tongue. Sew them together around the curved edges using a blanket stitch, leaving the flat edge unsewn.

Make 8.

Finishing the Pillow

1. Hem one 10½" side of each olive-green 10½" x 13" rectangle by folding ½" and stitching by machine. Hemming the wool isn't absolutely necessary, but without the hem, it may stretch out of shape when the pillow form is inserted into or removed from the finished pillow.

Machine Sewing Wool

Wool is thicker than cotton, so when sewing wool by machine, I use a walking foot so that the layers all feed easily and evenly under the presser foot.

2. Lay the appliquéd pillow front right side up. Place four tongues on each end of the pillow front, with right sides down and raw edges of the tongues aligned with the outside edge of the pillow. Baste the tongues to the pillow front by hand.

Baste.   Baste.

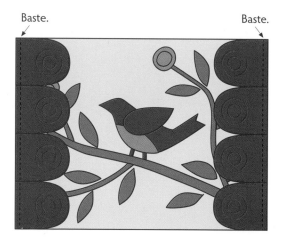

Vary the texture and thickness of the wools and include plaids as well as solids to add depth, interest, and character to your projects.

3. Place the two olive-green wool pieces on top of the pillow front with right sides facing down. Line up the sides so that the two hemmed edges overlap in the middle. Pin all the way around as shown at right, and sew the layers together using a ¼" seam allowance.

4. Turn the pillow right side out, and push out the corners. Insert the pillow form through the opening.

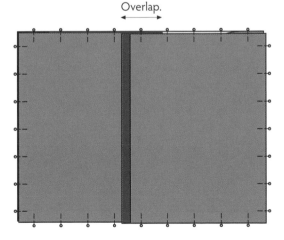

Overlap.

Winter Perch

Materials

All wool is hand dyed; piece sizes are based on wool that has been felted and is ready to use.

¼ yard of black print for border
¼ yard *each* of 2 red prints and 2 gold prints for blocks
⅛ yard of black print for block centers*
6" x 18" piece of brown-plaid wool for branches
7" x 14" piece of black wool for bird body
8" x 9" piece of olive-green wool for leaves
3" x 6" piece of gray textured wool for wing
2" x 6" piece of cream wool for berries
¼ yard of red floral stripe for binding
¾ yard of fabric for backing
25" x 32" piece of batting
Thread in colors to match appliqués**

You can use a scrap strip that is at least 2½" x 15".

**I used cotton quilting thread in matching colors.*

Cutting

From *each* red print, cut:
1 strip, 2" x 42"
1 strip, 2" x 14"

From the black print for block centers, cut:
1 strip, 2" x 14"

From *each* gold print, cut:
2 strips, 2" x 42"

From the black print for border, cut:
3 strips, 2" x 42"; crosscut into:
    2 strips, 2" x 15½"
    2 strips, 2" x 26"

From the red floral stripe, cut:
3 strips, 2¼" x 42"

I made this small quilt after noticing a group of birds perched in the tree outside my house last winter. I felt sad for them because the berries and leaves were all gone, so in my quilt, the quaint little bird has all the berries it needs, against a patchwork backdrop of simple Courthouse Steps blocks!

FINISHED WALL HANGING
26" x 18½"

FINISHED BLOCK
7½" x 7½"

Making the Blocks

1. Sew a red-print 2" x 14" strip to each side of the black-print 2" x 14" strip to make a strip set. Press seam allowances toward the black strip. Crosscut the strip set into six 2"-wide segments.

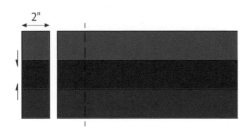

Cut 6 segments.

2. Sew the segments from step 1 to a gold-print 2" x 42" strip with right sides together, chain piecing them one after the other. Press the seam allowances toward the gold strip.

3. Repeat step 2 to chain piece the segments to a second gold-print strip on the other side. Press the seam allowances toward the gold strip.

4. Cut the units apart carefully with a ruler and rotary cutter. They should measure 5" x 5".

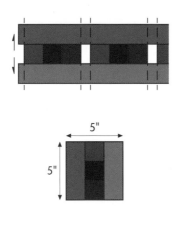

5. Repeat steps 2 and 3 to sew the units from step 4 to the red-print 2" x 42" strips. Press the seam allowances toward the red strips and cut apart into units that measure 5" x 8".

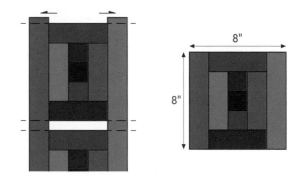

6. Repeat steps 2 and 3 to sew the units from step 5 to the remaining gold-print 2" x 42" strips and to the leftover gold strips from step 2. Cut apart into blocks that measure 8" x 8".

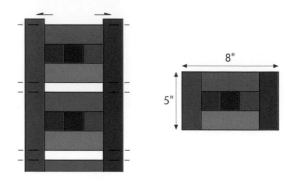

Assembling the Quilt

1. Lay out the blocks in two rows of three blocks each, rotating them as shown. Sew the blocks together in rows and press seam allowances as shown. Sew the rows together and press.

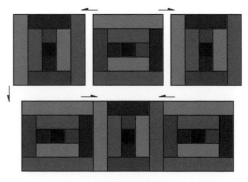

Quilt assembly

2. Sew a black-print 2" x 15½" strip to each short end of the quilt. Press the seam allowances toward the border. Sew the black-print 2" x 26" strips to the top and bottom and press.

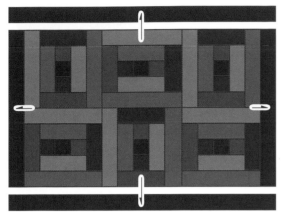

Adding borders

Appliquéing the Quilt Top

1. Referring to "Wool Appliqué" on page 70, cut out the appliqué shapes using the patterns for the bird, branches, leaves, and berries on pullout pattern sheet 2.

2. Position the appliqués on the quilt top, referring to the photograph on page 29 for placement. Pin or use fabric glue to tack them in place. Using matching thread and a whipstitch, appliqué the pieces to the quilt top.

Stitching Order

If a design includes any small pieces that lie on top of larger pieces, such as the wing on a bird, I like to stitch those shapes together before stitching the larger piece to the background. It's much easier to handle just one layer of wool at a time when stitching onto a cotton quilt top.

The closely spaced meander quilting makes the appliqués pop!

Finishing the Quilt

Refer to "Finishing" on page 77 and "Making a Label" on page 78 for additional information.

1. Layer the quilt top with batting and backing, and baste.

2. Hand or machine quilt as desired. I machine quilted my little quilt by first outlining all the wool pieces, and then close stippling on the rest of the quilt. I also like to add quilting to larger wool appliqué pieces such as the bird. I quilted flowing lines across its body and outlined the wing.

3. Trim the excess batting and backing.

4. Prepare and sew the binding to the quilt using the strips of red floral stripe.

5. Add a label to the back, especially if you plan to give the quilt as a gift.

Home Sweet Home
PENNY RUG

Warm up any room in your home with this wool penny rug, displaying it on the floor or on a table or other surface. This penny rug matches the hooked rug on page 35—it's for those who love the design, but prefer appliqué rather than rug hooking.

FINISHED RUG
24" x 24"

Designed by Jenifer Gaston, stitched by Janice Minear

Materials

All wool is hand dyed; piece sizes are based on wool that has been felted and is ready to use.

24" x 24" piece of mottled-tan wool for background
24" x 24" piece of coat-weight wool for backing
16" x 16" piece of mottled-brown wool for center background
12" x 18" piece of brown-plaid wool for wings, letters, numbers, roof, windows, and door
12" x 12" piece of olive-green wool for leaves and stems
8" x 14" piece of black wool for birds
9" x 9" piece of red wool for house
4" x 16" piece of blue-plaid wool for flowers
2" x 10" piece of orange wool for flowers
2" x 6" piece of robin's egg–blue wool for flower centers
3" x 4" piece of oatmeal wool for smoke
Wool thread in colors to match appliqués
Size 8 black pearl cotton

Appliquéing the Penny Rug

1. Referring to "Wool Appliqué" on page 70, cut out the appliqué shapes using the patterns for the birds, flowers, stems, leaves, house, smoke, letters, and numbers on pullout pattern sheet 3. Cut the stems on the bias before cutting the leaves.

2. Cut the corners of the brown-wool 16" x 16" square using the pattern on pullout pattern sheet 3. Center it on the tan wool 24" x 24" background and whipstitch in place.

3. For the flowers, sew the top layers to the middle layers, and then stitch the units to the bottom layer using a whipstitch. Stitch the windows and door to the house.

4. Arrange the remaining pieces on the background, referring to the placement guide at right and the photo above. Whipstitch all pieces with matching wool thread.

5. Stitch the line between the chimney and the house with black pearl cotton using a backstitch.

Finishing the Rug

Lay the penny rug on top of the wool 24" x 24" backing, with wrong sides together and raw edges aligned. Pin together, and then blanket stitch the edges all the way around.

Placement guide

Home Sweet Home
HOOKED RUG

What better way to warm up your home than with a hand-hooked rug? This is a great project for beginners, featuring a whimsical design that looks just as delightful on a table or wall as on the floor. By hand tearing strips of hand-dyed wool, you will instantly give your rug that old, much-loved look!

FINISHED RUG
24" x 24"

Materials

All wool is hand dyed; wool yardage and piece sizes are based on wool that has been felted and is ready to use.

¾ yard of mottled-brown wool for border
½ yard *total* of 3 black wools for center background
10" x 30" piece of red wool for house
10" x 30" piece of black wool for birds
8" x 30" piece of blue wool for flowers
8" x 30" piece of olive-green wool for stems and leaves
4" x 30" piece of black-plaid wool for wings
3" x 30" piece of brown-plaid wool for doors, windows, and roof
3" x 30" piece of light-brown-plaid wool for letters and numbers
2" x 30" piece of pumpkin wool for flowers
2" x 30" piece of teal wool for flower centers
1" x 30" piece of gray wool for smoke
32" x 32" piece of fabric for backing (linen, monk's cloth, or
    Scottish burlap)
3 yards of black rug-binding tape
Black Sharpie marker
1 yard of 54"-wide white nylon netting (tulle)
Sheet of paper at least 25" x 25"
Masking tape or blue painter's tape
Rug-hooking frame or sturdy quilting hoop
Primitive rug hook

Finishing Option

Instead of using binding tape as I've done for "Home Sweet Home," you can make a self-binding with the extra backing fabric. Allow an extra 2" when trimming the backing. Fold the edge over 1" and then fold again and whipstitch the edge to the back of the rug, mitering the corners as you get to them.

Transferring the Pattern

1. Trace the patterns on pullout pattern sheet 3 onto a large sheet of paper to make a complete full-sized pattern, referring to the placement guide below. Begin by tracing the center background area, and then add the individual designs for the house, flowers, and birds. Add letters and numbers for initials and the date as desired.

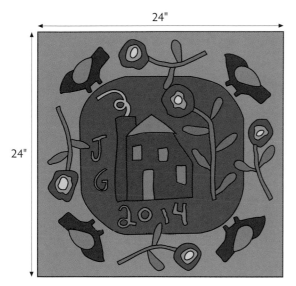

Placement guide

2. Cut a piece of nylon netting the same size as the backing fabric and pin it to the paper pattern with straight pins. Trace the lines with the Sharpie marker.

3. Machine stitch around the edges of the backing fabric with a zigzag stitch to prevent fraying.

4. Tape the backing fabric to a flat surface with masking tape or painter's tape. With the Sharpie marker and a ruler, draw a 24" square in the center of the backing, making sure to keep the drawn square on the grain line of the fabric. Then place the nylon netting on the backing, and pin in place. Trace over all of the lines with the marker to transfer the pattern to the backing.

Cutting Wool Strips

I like to hand cut and tear my wool strips to give my rugs an older, primitive look. You can use a strip cutter specifically designed for rug hooking if you have access to one. You can also use a rotary cutter, mat, and ruler to cut strips.

1. To tear strips, make small cuts into the edge of the wool about every ½" and then tear them. If I want narrower strips for smaller details, I cut the ½" strips in half with scissors to make ¼"-wide strips.

2. Cut strips as you go. That way you won't cut more than you need and the strips won't become tangled up with each other.

Hooking the Rug

If you're new to rug hooking, read "Rug-Hooking Basics" on page 38 for additional details.

1. Stretch the backing with the pattern transferred on it into a sturdy hoop or rug-hooking frame. It should be fairly tight, but you don't need to be able to bounce a quarter off of it!

2. Hook the designs within the rug first: house, flowers, birds, letters, and numbers. If you are a beginner, practice hooking the border lines first.

3. Hook the perimeter of the rug with the mottled-brown strips.

4. Hook the perimeter of the center section with the black strips. Then hook around each item in the center section. Fill in the spaces after outlining the individual shapes.

5. Hook an outline around each item in the border a couple of times. Then fill in the rest of the border.

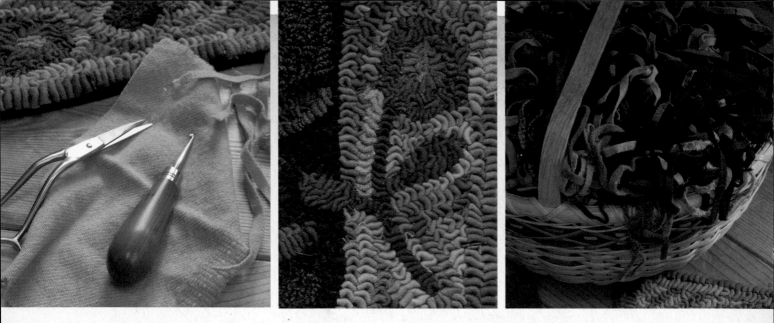

Rug-Hooking Basics

Rug hooks come in many styles, but if you're a beginner, try an inexpensive one made for primitive rug hooking to get the hang of it. Hold your hook as you would a pencil, or with the handle in the palm of your hand, as if you were eating soup with bad manners!

Generally, if you are just starting out, it's a good idea to practice hooking around the border of the rug. This has the benefit of holding the shape of the rug as you hook. Once you have gone around at least once, you can move to the center and begin the fun parts, such as the house and flowers.

1. With your left hand (if you're right-handed), hold a strip of wool beneath the backing. With your right hand, insert the hook down through an opening in the weave of the backing fabric. With your left hand, place the wool strip onto the hook and pull it back up to the top with your right hand, leaving about ½" of the strip end on top.

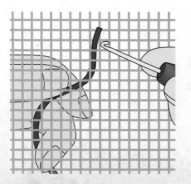

2. Push the hook back down through the backing, a couple of threads away, and catch the strip again, this time only pulling up a loop. The rule of thumb is that the loops should be as high as the width of the majority of your strips. For example, if your strips are ½" wide, the loops should be ½" high. While pulling up loops, be sure to pull up any slack from the strip below so that the back of the rug doesn't also have loops. You want the back to be nice and flat.

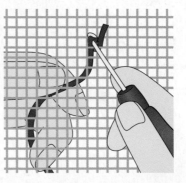

3. Start by outlining objects, hooking within the drawn lines to keep them from growing larger than they should be. Once the shapes are outlined, you can fill them in by hooking from the outline toward the center, going around and around within the shapes. When hooking a row next to another row, you want the loops to just touch, like soldiers touching shoulders, rather than crowding each

other out and ending up too packed. Make sure to leave one or two holes open in the background fabric between rows to prevent overcrowding.

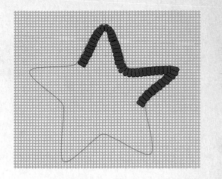

Hook inside the drawn lines.

4. Once all the shapes are hooked, use the background wool to outline around each shape a couple of times, and then hook the background. I like to hook in sections, adding movement by hooking curved shapes.

5. The object is to make the loops as even as you can. When you end one strip, begin the next strip in the same hole as the ending tail and continue hooking. All strip ends—beginning and ending—should be on top of the rug and need to be trimmed off evenly with the height of the loops.

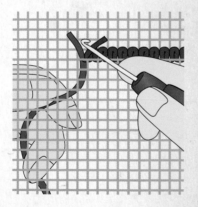

Finishing the Rug

After your rug is completely hooked, press it with steam to allow the fibers to settle in and make everything look nice and uniform.

1. Fold a large terry-cloth towel and place it on your ironing board or surface. Place the rug on the towel, wrong side up.

2. Wet a kitchen tea towel and wring most of the water out. Lay the damp towel on the back of the rug.

3. With your iron on the wool and steam setting, press the back of the rug, lifting and placing the iron on each section and pressing for about 10 seconds in each area. You may have to re-wet and move the towel around to press the entire rug.

4. Flip the rug over and repeat the pressing process on the front of the rug, but use less pressure this time. Lay the rug flat and allow it to dry overnight.

5. Cut away the excess backing fabric, leaving about 1" from the hooking. Cut the corners at an angle, and zigzag stitch or serge the edges to prevent them from fraying.

6. Fold the excess fabric to the back of the rug and baste it in place with a strong thread such as hand-quilting thread.

7. Place the binding tape on the back of the rug, aligning it with the edge of the rug. With strong black thread, whipstitch the outer edge of the binding as close as possible to the last row of hooking all the way around the rug. When you get to the beginning, overlap the edges, trim the excess, and fold the top edge under and stitch in place.

8. Stitch the inner edge of the binding to the back of the rug with either a running stitch or a whipstitch. When you come to a corner, fold, miter, and stitch in place.

Simple Folk Sampler

I have always been drawn to antique folk-art samplers, so I gathered up a handful of my favorite pieced blocks and created a few simple appliquéd blocks to add to the mix. Set on point, the blocks are surrounded by fun folksy appliqués in the border!

FINISHED QUILT
25½" x 34"

FINISHED BLOCK
6" x 6"

Designed, pieced, and appliquéd by Jenifer Gaston, quilted by Darlene Szabo of Sew Graceful Quilting

Materials

1 yard of black print for setting triangles and border
20 squares, 10" x 10", of assorted medium to dark prints (blues, greens, reds, oranges, browns, and blacks) for blocks and appliqués
8 squares, 10" x 10", of assorted light prints for block backgrounds
⅜ yard of black stripe for binding
1 yard of fabric for backing
31" x 40" piece of batting
Thread in colors to match appliqués
Size 8 pearl cotton in black and brown

Cutting

Choose from the assorted light, medium, and dark 10" squares when cutting the blocks.

APPLIQUÉ BLOCKS

From *each* of 3 light prints, cut:
1 square, 7" x 7"

BASKET BLOCK

From 1 light print, cut:
5 squares, 2⅜" x 2⅜"; cut 1 square in half diagonally to make 2 triangles
2 rectangles, 2" x 3½"
1 square, 3⅞" x 3⅞"; cut in half diagonally to make 2 triangles (1 is extra)

From 1 blue print, cut:
2 squares, 2⅜" x 2⅜"

From 1 orange print, cut:
2 squares, 2⅜" x 2⅜"

Continued on page 42

Continued from page 40

From 1 brown print, cut:
1 square, 2⅜" x 2⅜"; cut in half diagonally
    to make 2 triangles
1 square, 3⅞" x 3⅞"; cut in half diagonally
    to make 2 triangles (1 is extra)

VARIABLE STAR BLOCK

From 1 light print, cut:
4 squares, 2" x 2"
1 square, 4¼" x 4¼"

From 1 red print, cut:
4 squares, 2⅜" x 2⅜"

From 1 blue print, cut:
1 square, 3½" x 3½"

SHOOFLY BLOCK

From 1 red print, cut:
1 square, 2½" x 2½"
2 squares, 2⅞" x 2⅞"

From 1 light print, cut:
4 squares, 2½" x 2½"
2 squares, 2⅞" x 2⅞"

STAR PUZZLE BLOCK

From 1 light print, cut:
4 rectangles, 2" x 3½"
2 squares, 2⅜" x 2⅜"

From 1 red print, cut:
4 squares, 2" x 2"
2 squares, 2⅜" x 2⅜"

From 1 blue print, cut:
4 squares, 2" x 2"
2 squares, 2⅜" x 2⅜"

From 1 black print, cut:
2 squares, 2⅜" x 2⅜"

DUTCHMAN'S PUZZLE BLOCK

From 1 light print, cut:
8 squares, 2⅜" x 2⅜"

From 1 orange print, cut:
1 square, 4¼" x 4¼"

From 1 green print, cut:
1 square, 4¼" x 4¼"

SETTING TRIANGLES, BORDERS, AND BINDING

From the black print, cut:
4 strips, 4½" x 42"
2 squares, 10" x 10"; cut into quarters diagonally
    to make 8 triangles (2 are extra)
2 squares, 5½" x 5½"; cut in half diagonally to
    make 4 triangles

From the black stripe, cut:
4 strips, 2¼" x 42"

Making the Appliqué Blocks

Refer to "Needle-Turn Appliqué" on page 75 or use your own favorite method. All appliqué patterns are on pullout pattern sheet 4.

1. Prepare the bird, branch, flowers, and leaves.

2. Position and appliqué the shapes to one of the light 7" squares using the pattern for placement guidance.

3. Embroider the stems using the stem stitch and two strands of brown pearl cotton. Backstitch the legs with black pearl cotton. Refer to "Embroidery Stitches" on page 71 as needed.

Appliqué placement

4. Repeat steps 1 and 2 using the patterns for the Rosebud block.

Appliqué placement

5. Repeat steps 1 and 2 using the patterns for the Sunflower block.

Appliqué placement

6. Trim and square up the blocks to measure 6½" x 6½".

Making the Basket Block

1. Draw a diagonal line from corner to corner on the wrong side of four light 2⅜" squares.

2. Place two of the marked squares right sides together with two orange 2⅜" squares. Sew ¼" from each side of the drawn lines. Cut on the drawn lines and press seam allowances toward the darker fabric. This will make four identical half-square-triangle units. One will be extra.

Make 4.

43

3. Repeat step 2 with the remaining marked light squares and two blue 2⅜" squares to make four identical half-square-triangle units. One will be extra.

Make 4.

4. Sew a brown-print 2⅜" triangle to one end of a light 2" x 3½" rectangle, and press toward the brown triangle. Make two as shown.

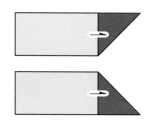

5. Arrange the half-square-triangle units from steps 2 and 3 and the two light 2⅜" triangles in three rows as shown. Sew the units into rows and press seam allowances in opposite directions from row to row. Sew the rows together and press in one direction.

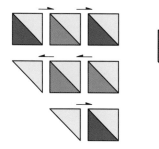
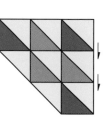

6. Sew a brown-print 3⅞" triangle to the lower-left corner of the unit from step 5. Press seam allowances toward the brown triangle.

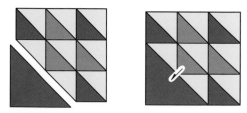

7. Sew the rectangle units from step 4 to the left and bottom edges of the unit from step 6. Press the seam allowances toward the rectangles. Sew a light 3⅞" triangle to the lower-left corner. Press.

Making the Variable Star Block

1. Referring to "Flying-Geese Units" Method 2 on page 74, make four matching units using four red 2⅜" squares and the light 4¼" square.

Make 4.

2. Arrange the flying-geese units, four light 2" squares, and the blue-print 3½" square as shown. Sew the units into rows and press as indicated by the arrows. Sew the rows together and press. The block should measure 6½" x 6½".

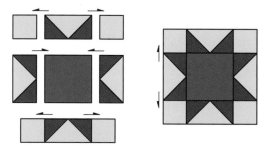

Making the Shoofly Block

1. Draw a diagonal line from corner to corner on the wrong side of two light 2⅞" squares.

2. Place the marked squares right sides together with two red 2⅞" squares. Sew ¼" from each side of the drawn lines. Cut on the drawn lines and press seam allowances toward the red fabric. This will make four identical half-square-triangle units.

Make 4.

3. Lay out the half-square-triangle units, four light 2½" squares, and one red 2½" square in three rows as shown. Sew together into rows and press seam allowances toward the red. Sew the rows together and press. The block should measure 6½" x 6½".

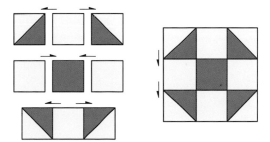

Making the Star Puzzle Block

1. Referring to "Flying-Geese Units" on page 74, use method 1 to draw a diagonal line from corner to corner on the wrong side of each red and blue 2" square.

2. Align a marked red square on the left end of a light 2" x 3½" rectangle. Sew on the drawn line. Cut away the outer part of the red square, leaving a ¼" seam allowance and the light

rectangle below intact. Press toward the outer corner. Make four of these units.

3. Repeat step 2 to sew a blue 2" square to the opposite end of each light rectangle, making four flying-geese units with one red and one blue point.

Make 4.

4. Draw a diagonal line from corner to corner on the wrong side of two blue 2⅜" squares and two light 2⅜" squares. Place the blue squares right sides together with two red 2⅜" squares and place the light squares right sides together with two black 2⅜" squares. Sew ¼" from the drawn lines on both sides. Cut on the drawn lines, and press seam allowances toward the darker fabrics.

Make 4 of each.

5. Sew the four blue-and-red half-square-triangle units together to make a pinwheel unit for the block center.

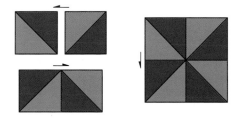

6. Lay out the flying-geese units, the half-square-triangle units, and the pinwheel unit in three rows as shown. Sew the units into rows and press seam allowances as indicated by the arrows. Sew the rows together and press. The block should measure 6½" x 6½".

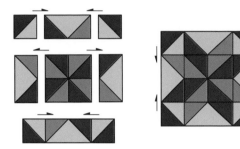

Making the Dutchman's Puzzle Block

1. Referring to "Flying-Geese Units" on page 74, use method 2 to make four matching units using one orange 4¼" square and four light 2⅜" squares. For these flying geese, press the seam allowances toward the light fabric.

Make 4.

2. Repeat step 1 to make four matching flying-geese units using one green 4¼" square and four light 2⅜" squares.

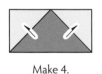

Make 4.

3. Lay out the eight flying-geese units as shown and sew together in pairs. Press seam allowances as indicated by the arrows. Sew the pairs together and press to make the block.

You'll have an orange pinwheel in the center. The block should measure 6½" x 6½".

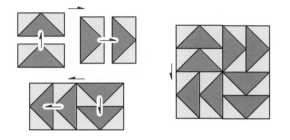

Assembling the Quilt

1. Lay out the blocks, side setting triangles, and corner triangles in diagonal rows as shown in the assembly diagram on page 47. Sew the blocks into diagonal rows and press as indicated by the arrows. Sew the rows together and press seam allowances in one direction. Note that the setting triangles are cut oversized and will be trimmed in the next step.

2. Trim all four sides with a long ruler and rotary cutter to square up the quilt, leaving a ¼" seam allowance beyond the points of the blocks.

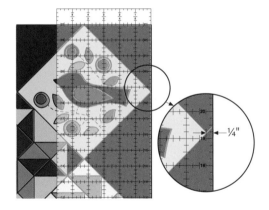

3. Measure the length of the quilt top through the center. Cut two black-print 4½"-wide strips to that measurement and sew the strips to the sides of the quilt. Press seam allowances toward the border.

Darlene stitched simple quilting to set off the blocks and added beautiful echo quilting around the appliqués in the border.

4. Measure the width of the quilt top through the center and cut two black-print 4½"-wide strips to that measurement. Sew the strips to the top and bottom of the quilt, and press.

Quilt assembly

5. Using the border patterns for the bird, sunflowers, and flower buds on pullout pattern sheet 4, prepare the appliqués from the remainder of the assorted prints. Position the appliqués throughout the border using the photograph on page 41 as a guide. Stitch the appliqués in place.

Finishing the Quilt

Refer to "Finishing" on page 77 and "Making a Label" on page 78 for additional information.

1. Layer the quilt top with batting and backing, and baste.

2. Hand or machine quilt as desired. The quilt shown features echo quilting around the border appliqués and custom designs within each block.

3. Trim the excess batting and backing.

4. Prepare and sew the binding to the quilt using the black stripe 2¼"-wide strips.

5. Add a label to the back, especially if you plan to give the quilt as a gift.

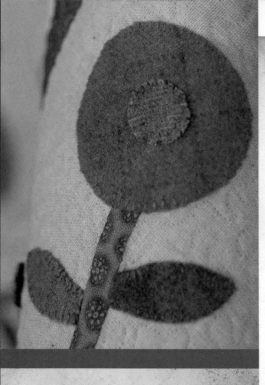

Water the Flowers

I can never have enough flowers blooming in my garden, but remembering to water them is a challenge. Maybe hanging this watering can quilt on the wall will remind me every day to do just that!

FINISHED WALL HANGING
44½" x 44½"

Designed, pieced, and appliquéd by Jenifer Gaston, quilted by Brian D. McCoy of Bolts and Quarters Quilt Shop

Materials

All wool is hand dyed; piece sizes are based on wool that has been felted and is ready to use. Cotton yardage is based on 42"-wide fabric.

1⅝ yards of tan osnaburg fabric or other woven cotton for appliqué background, pieced border, and fourth border

½ yard of gray print for watering can and third border

⅓ yard of solid-red woven fabric for first border, pieced border, and Nine Patch blocks

1 fat quarter (18" x 21") of green print for bias stems and vines

1 fat eighth (9" x 21") *each* of 6 medium/dark woven fabrics for pieced border and Nine Patch blocks

1 fat eighth (9" x 21") *each* of 3 light woven fabrics for pieced border and Nine Patch blocks

7" x 18" piece *each* of 2 pumpkin plaid wools for flowers

5" x 25" piece of green wool for leaves and flower centers

2" x 20" piece of red wool for berries

2" x 16" piece of dark-green wool for leaves

2" x 6" piece of striped wool for watering can accent

½ yard of blue stripe for binding

3 yards of fabric for backing

51" x 51" piece of batting

Wool thread in colors to match appliqués

Size 8 green pearl cotton for embroidery

Water-soluble marking tool

⅜" bias-tape maker (optional)

Cutting

From the osnaburg, cut:
4 strips, 7" x 42"; crosscut into 4 strips, 7" x 32½"
1 strip, 2½" x 21"
1 square, 22" x 22"

Continued on page 50

Continued from page 48

From the green print, cut:
6 bias strips, ⅞" x approximately 20"
4 bias strips, ⅞" x approximately 9"

From the red woven fabric, cut:
1 strip, 2½" x 42"; crosscut into:
    1 strip, 2½" x 21"
    4 squares, 2½" x 2½"
4 strips, 1½" x 42"; crosscut into:
    2 strips, 1½" x 20½"
    2 strips, 1½" x 22½"

From the 3 light woven fabrics, cut *a total of*:
6 strips, 2½" x 21"
16 squares, 2½" x 2½"

**From the 6 medium/dark woven fabrics,
cut *a total of*:**
6 strips, 2½" x 21"
16 squares, 2½" x 2½"

From the gray print, cut:
4 strips, 1½" x 42"; crosscut into:
    2 strips, 1½" x 30½"
    2 strips, 1½" x 32½"

From the blue stripe, cut:
5 strips, 2¼" x 42"

Appliquéing the Quilt Center

1. Zigzag stitch around the edge of the osnaburg 22" square to prevent fraying while you work.

2. Referring to "Needle-Turn Appliqué" on page 75, prepare the appliqués for the watering can using the patterns on pullout pattern sheet 2.

3. Referring to "Wool Appliqué" on page 70, cut out the appliqué shapes using the patterns for the flowers, leaves, and berries on pullout pattern sheet 2.

4. Refer to "Making Bias Stems and Vines" on page 76 to prepare the four ⅞" x 9" bias strips for the stems.

5. Position the appliqué shapes on the osnaburg square, referring to the placement diagram and the photo on page 49. Trim excess from the bias stems as needed. Pin and appliqué the pieces in place using your preferred method for the cotton pieces and a whipstitch for the wool pieces.

6. With your marker or pencil, draw the stem lines for the berry sprigs using the photo as a guide, but remember, they don't have to be perfect. Embroider the lines with pearl cotton and a stem stitch or backstitch.

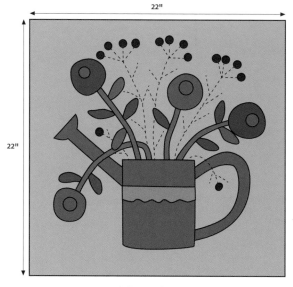

Appliqué placement

7. Remove any marks as needed, press the piece from the wrong side, and then trim the block to 20½" x 20½".

Adding the Borders

1. Sew a red woven 1½" x 20½" strip to each side of the appliquéd quilt center. Press the seam allowances toward the red. Sew the red woven 1½" x 22½" strips to the top and bottom and press in the same manner.

2. Sew a light 2½" x 21" strip to a medium or dark 2½" x 21" strip to make a strip set. Press the seam allowance toward the darker fabric. Make seven strip sets, including the red 2½" x 21" strip and the osnaburg 2½" x 21" strip. Cut the strip sets into 2½"-wide segments. You will need 52 segments.

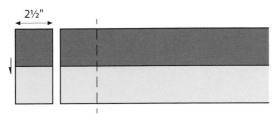

Make 7 strip sets.
Cut 52 segments.

3. Sew 11 segments together to make a checkerboard strip for the side of the appliquéd center. Make two. Sew 15 segments together to make a top checkerboard strip. Repeat to make a 15-segment bottom strip.

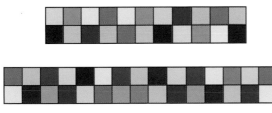

Make 2 of each.

4. Sew the shorter checkerboard strips to the sides of the quilt center. Press seam allowances toward the red border. Sew the longer checkerboard strips to the top and bottom and press.

5. Sew the gray-print 1½" x 30½" strips to the sides of the quilt. Press seam allowances toward the gray strips. Sew the gray-print 1½" x 32½" strips to the top and bottom of the quilt, and press seam allowances toward the gray strips.

6. Sew an osnaburg 7" x 32½" strip to each side of the quilt. Press seam allowances toward the gray border. Zigzag stitch the long raw edges of the osnaburg to help minimize fraying.

7. Arrange a red 2½" square, four light 2½" squares, and four medium or dark 2½" squares into rows to make a Nine Patch block as shown. Sew the squares into rows and press seam allowances toward the darker squares. Sew the rows together and press to make the block. Make four Nine Patch blocks.

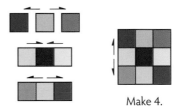

Make 4.

8. Sew Nine Patch blocks to opposite ends of the remaining osnaburg 7" x 32½" strips, aligning the block with the side that will be sewn to the quilt. There will be an extra ½" on the outer side of the osnaburg strips. Press seam allowances toward the Nine Patch blocks.

9. Sew the strips to the top and bottom of the quilt, and press seam allowances toward the gray border.

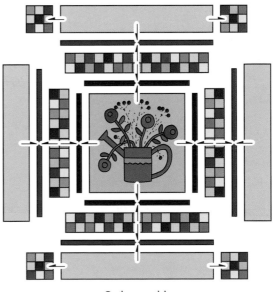

Quilt assembly

Appliquéing the Borders

1. Sew the six green ⅞" x 20" bias strips together with diagonal seams, referring to "Making Bias Stems and Vines" as needed.

2. Cut the bias vine into four lengths, about 28" long, one for each side of the quilt.

3. Prepare the wool appliqués using the patterns for the flowers, leaves, and berries on pullout pattern sheet 2. Whipstitch the flower centers to the flowers.

4. Position the vine, flowers, and leaves on the border, referring to the photograph for placement guidance. Trim the bias vines if needed and stitch in place.

5. Mark the stem lines for the berry sprigs with the marker, and embroider them with the green pearl cotton and a stem stitch.

Finishing the Quilt

Refer to "Finishing" on page 77 and "Making a Label" on page 78 for additional information.

1. Layer the quilt top with batting and backing, and baste.

2. Hand or machine quilt as desired. The appliqués in my quilt were outline quilted and the space around them filled with close stipple quilting.

3. Trim the excess batting and backing.

4. Prepare and sew the binding to the quilt using the strips of blue stripe.

5. Add a label to the back, especially if you plan to give the quilt as a gift.

Flower Vines

Materials

All wool is hand dyed; piece sizes are based on wool that has been felted and is ready to use. Cotton yardage is based on 42"-wide fabric.

½ yard of tan textured woven fabric for appliqué background*
¼ yard of black print for Pinwheel blocks
¼ yard of red print for Pinwheel blocks
1 fat quarter (18" x 21") of light-brown print for bias vine and stems
⅛ yard *each* of red, gray, blue, and brown prints for Four Patch blocks
8" x 10" piece of light-green plaid wool for flowers
6" x 10" piece of green wool for leaves
6" x 10" piece of brown wool for leaves
6" x 8" piece of neutral plaid wool for leaves
6" x 8" piece of red wool for flowers
⅓ yard of tan stripe for binding
1⅝ yards of fabric for backing
21" x 55" piece of batting
⅜" bias-tape maker (optional)

*If you prefer not to piece the background, you'll need 1½ yards.

Cutting

From the red print, cut:
2 strips, 3" x 42"; cut into 24 squares, 3" x 3"

From the black print, cut:
2 strips, 3" x 42"; cut into 24 squares, 3" x 3"

From *each* of the 4 prints, cut:
1 strip, 2½" x 42"; cut into 12 squares, 2½" x 2½"

From the tan fabric, cut:*
2 strips, 6½" x 42"

From the light-brown print, cut:
3 bias strips, ⅞" x 15"
6 bias strips, ⅞" x 5"

From the tan stripe, cut:
4 strips, 2¼" x 42"

*If you purchased extra yardage, cut 1 strip, 6½" x 48½", from the lengthwise grain.

*T*here's nothing prettier than flowering vines added to simple patchwork. Contrasting Pinwheel and Four Patch blocks are complemented by both the appliqué and the texture of the woven background. This runner will go together quickly, so why not make one for your table and one for a friend?

FINISHED RUNNER
14½" x 48½"

FINISHED BLOCK
4" x 4"

Making the Blocks

1. Draw a diagonal line from corner to corner on the wrong side of each red-print 3" square. Layer a marked red square right sides together with a black-print 3" square. Sew ¼" from each side of the drawn line; cut on the line, and press seam allowances toward the black print. Trim and square the half-square-triangle unit to 2½" x 2½". Make 48.

Make 48.

2. Arrange four half-square-triangle units as shown to make the Pinwheel block. Sew together in rows; press seam allowances in opposite directions. Sew the rows together and press. Make 12 blocks.

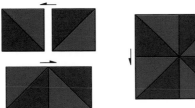

Make 12.

3. Arrange and sew one 2½" square each of red, gray, blue, and brown print to make a Four Patch block. Make 12 blocks.

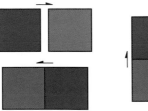

Make 12.

4. Sew two tan 6½" x 42" strips together end to end. Trim to make one strip, 48½" long.

5. Sew six Pinwheel blocks and six Four Patch blocks together to make a row. Press seam allowances toward the Four Patch blocks. Make two rows.

Make 2.

6. Sew a block row to each side of the tan 6½" x 48½" strip; press seam allowances toward the center.

Appliquéing the Runner Center

1. Sew the three light-brown ⅞" x 15" bias strips together with a diagonal seam to make one long strip. Refer to "Making Bias Stems and Vines" on page 76 to prepare the long strip for the vine and the ⅞" x 5" bias strips for the flower stems.

2. Referring to "Wool Appliqué" on page 70, cut out the appliqué shapes using the patterns for the leaves and flowers on pullout pattern sheet 4.

3. Position the long vine in the center of the table runner, curving it and pinning to keep it in place. Trim excess length as needed.

4. Place the shorter bias strips along the vine for the flower stems, referring to the assembly diagram for placement. Pin in place and tuck the ends under the main vine. Trim extra length as needed.

5. Place the wool flowers and leaves on the runner, and tack in place. Whipstitch with matching wool threads on the wool. Stitch the vine with cotton thread and a blind stitch.

Finishing the Runner

Refer to "Finishing" on page 77 and "Making a Label" on page 78 for additional information.

1. Layer the quilt top with batting and backing, and baste.

2. Hand or machine quilt as desired. I stitched tight stippling around the appliqués and all over the remainder of the table runner.

3. Trim the excess batting and backing.

4. Prepare and sew the binding to the table runner using the tan stripe 2¼"-wide strips.

5. Add a label to the back, especially if you plan to give the quilt as a gift.

Using lots of different wool plaids for the appliqués keeps it from looking flat and doesn't detract from the gracefulness of the design.

Pumpkin Harvest

*E*njoy a charming penny rug full of the beautiful autumn colors we all love. It's quick to stitch and can be enjoyed all season—from the first signs of fall until the Thanksgiving leftovers are gone.

FINISHED RUG
9" x 25½"

Designed by Jenifer Gaston, stitched by Carolyn Curfman

Materials

All wool is hand dyed; piece sizes are based on wool that has been felted and is ready to use. Cotton yardage is based on 42"-wide fabric.

10" x 36" piece of olive-green plaid wool for background and tongues
12" x 12" piece of brown-plaid wool for vine and stem
7" x 12" piece of orange-plaid wool for pumpkin
8" x 10" piece of gold wool for star, penny circles, and leaf
4" x 12" piece of purple-plaid wool for penny circles and leaves
5" x 9" piece of black wool for bird
5" x 5" piece of red wool for leaves
4" x 5½" piece of orange wool for pumpkin center
2" x 5" piece of black-plaid wool for wing
2½" x 4" piece of rust wool for leaf
⅜ yard of homespun fabric for backing
Wool thread in colors to match appliqués

Cutting

From the olive-green plaid wool, cut:
1 rectangle, 9" x 20"
12 tongues using the pattern on pullout sheet 4

From the brown-plaid wool, cut:
1 bias strip, ¼" x 16"

From the homespun, cut:
1 rectangle, 10" x 21"

Appliquéing the Background

1. Referring to "Wool Appliqué" on page 70, cut out the appliqué shapes using the patterns for the pumpkin, bird, leaves, star, and penny circles on pullout pattern sheet 4.

2. Position the pumpkin, leaves, bird, and star on the olive-green 9" x 20" rectangle. Refer to the placement guide and the photo on page 58. Use pins or dots of fabric glue to hold the pieces in place. Whipstitch with wool thread, matching colors to the appliqué pieces. Whipstitch the brown-plaid bias strip

to the pumpkin and background, curling and looping it to create the vine.

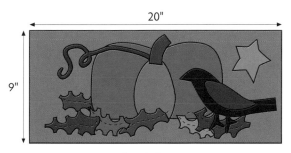

20"

9"

Appliqué placement

3. Stitch large running stitches through the center of the leaves with contrasting colors of wool thread. Where stems are needed on leaves, use a backstitch or stem stitch with dark-brown wool thread. Make an eye on the bird with a French knot.

4. Stitch a small penny circle onto a large circle using a whipstitch. Make six and then stitch each one to a brown-plaid tongue.

5. Layer an appliquéd tongue on a plain tongue and stitch around the curved edges, using a blanket stitch to hold them together. You don't need to stitch the straight edges.

Assembling the Rug

1. Turn the raw edges of the homespun 10" x 21" rectangle under ½" and press well.

2. Place the appliquéd piece on top of the homespun with wrong sides together. Sandwich the tongues between the layers on both ends, making sure the pennies are facing up. Pin together, and baste the tongues in place so that you can remove the pins.

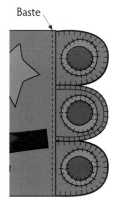

Baste

3. Blanket-stitch all the way around the entire piece, catching the tongues as you stitch. Be sure to go all the way through the tongues so that they will be secure on the back as well.

Baskets a-Plenty

*S*nuggly-soft woven fabrics in soothing, subtle colors make this basket quilt a favorite to cuddle under on chilly days. The wonderful textured fabrics are woven cottons from Diamond Textiles. They add depth and character reminiscent of vintage homespun fabrics.

FINISHED QUILT
65½" x 82½"

FINISHED BLOCK
12" x 12"

Designed by Jenifer Gaston, pieced by Vicki Lough, quilted by Jill Churchill of Ta Da Quilting Studio

Materials

Yardage is based on 42"-wide fabric.

3½ yards of light-blue stripe for alternate blocks, setting triangles, and outer border
1 yard of dark-blue stripe for inner border and binding
⅔ yard of brown check for baskets
⅜ yard *each* of 6 light fabrics for basket backgrounds
⅓ yard *each* of 2 dark-blue fabrics for blocks
⅓ yard of rust fabric for blocks
5 yards of fabric for backing
72" x 89" piece of batting

Cutting

From *each* of the light fabrics, cut:
1 strip, 6⅞" x 42"; crosscut:
    1 square, 6⅞" x 6⅞"; cut in half diagonally to make 2 triangles
    4 rectangles, 3½" x 6½"
1 strip, 4" x 42"; crosscut into:
    6 squares, 4" x 4"
    2 squares, 3⅞" x 3⅞"; cut in half diagonally to make 4 triangles

From *each* of the dark-blue fabrics, cut:
2 strips, 4" x 42"; crosscut into 12 squares, 4" x 4"

From the rust fabric, cut:
2 strips, 4" x 42"; crosscut into 12 squares, 4" x 4"

From the brown check, cut:
2 strips, 6⅞" x 42"; crosscut 6 squares, 6⅞" x 6⅞". Cut in half diagonally to make 12 triangles.
2 strips, 3⅞" x 42"; crosscut 12 squares, 3⅞" x 3⅞". Cut in half diagonally to make 24 triangles.

From the light-blue stripe, cut:
3 squares, 18½" x 18½"; cut into quarters diagonally to make 12 triangles (2 are extra)
2 squares, 9¾" x 9¾"; cut in half diagonally to make 4 triangles

Continued on page 62

Continued from page 60

**From the remainder of the light-blue stripe,
cut *on the lengthwise grain:***
4 strips, 6½" x 72"
6 squares, 12½" x 12½"

From the dark-blue stripe, cut:
7 strips, 1½" x 42"
8 strips, 2¼" x 42"

Making the Blocks

1. Draw a diagonal line on the wrong side of the three matching light 4" squares. Layer a marked square right sides together with one of each blue 4" square and one rust 4" square. Sew ¼" from each side of the drawn line. Cut on the drawn line, and press seam allowances toward the darker fabric. You will have two of each blue and two rust half-square-triangle units.

Make 2 of each.

2. Trim and square up the half-square-triangle units to measure 3½" x 3½".

3. Select two light 3½" x 6½" rectangles that match the light fabric used in step 1. Sew a brown-check 3⅞" triangle to one end of each rectangle as shown, making sure the triangles are angled in opposite directions.

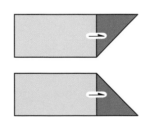

4. Arrange the half-square-triangle units from step 2 and two matching light 3⅞" triangles in three rows as shown. Sew the units into rows and press seam allowances in opposite directions from row to row. Sew the rows together and press as indicated by the arrows.

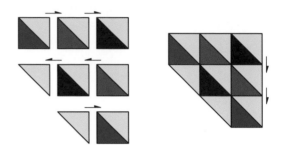

5. Sew a brown-check 6⅞" triangle to the lower-left corner of the unit from step 4. Press seam allowances toward the brown triangle.

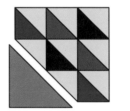

6. Sew the rectangle units from step 3 to the left and bottom edges of the unit from step 5. Press seam allowances toward the rectangles. Sew a matching light 6⅞" triangle to the lower-left corner. Press.

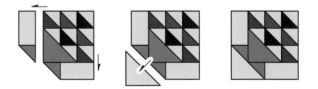

7. Repeat steps 1–6 to make a total of 12 Basket blocks.

Assembling the Quilt

1. Arrange the blocks and light-blue setting squares in diagonal rows as shown in the quilt assembly diagram. Add the side and corner setting triangles.

2. Sew the blocks together in rows and press seam allowances toward the setting squares and triangles. Sew the rows together and press seam allowances in one direction. Add the corner triangles last and press toward the triangles.

Quilt assembly

3. Use a long ruler and rotary cutter to square up the corners and trim the sides, making sure to leave a ¼" seam allowance outside the block points.

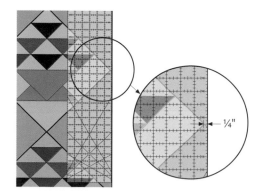

4. Sew the dark-blue striped 1½" x 42" strips together end to end to make one long strip. Press seam allowances to one side.

5. Measure the length of the quilt top through the middle and cut two border strips to that measurement. Sew one to each side of the quilt. Press seam allowances toward the border.

6. Measure the width of the quilt through the middle, including the borders just added. Cut two dark-blue border strips to that measurement and sew these to the top and bottom of the quilt. Press.

7. Repeat steps 5 and 6 to measure, trim, and add the light-blue 6½"-wide strips to the quilt for the outer border.

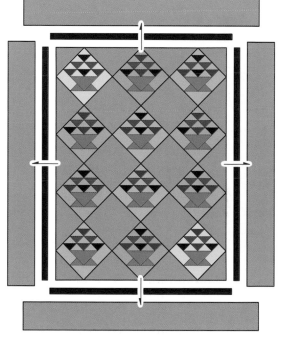

Adding borders

Better Borders

When sewing inner-border strips to the center of the quilt, you may find it's more accurate to sew with the border strip on top. If there has been any stretching along the sides of the quilt, the feed dogs will gently ease it to fit the measured border strip.

Finishing the Quilt

Refer to "Finishing" on page 77 and "Making a Label" on page 78 for additional information.

1. Layer the quilt top with batting and backing, and baste.

2. Hand or machine quilt as desired. The quilt shown includes flowers, vines, and leaves, a nice complement to the subtle fabrics.

3. Trim the excess batting and backing.

4. Prepare and sew the binding to the quilt using the dark-blue stripe 2¼"-wide strips.

5. Add a label to the back, especially if you plan to give the quilt as a gift.

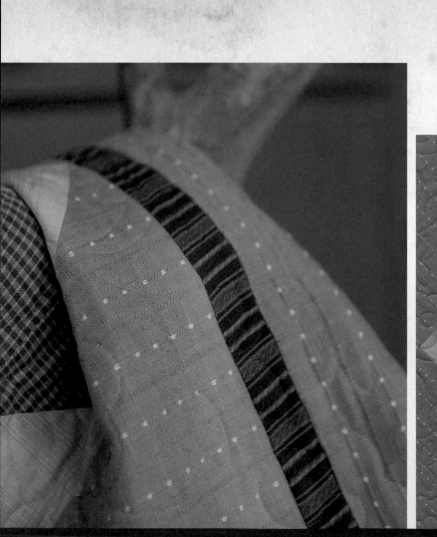

Cousin/quilter, Jill Churchill, quilted a simple allover floral design to complement the quilt.

Churning Stars

*E*njoy scrappy blocks that are a breeze to make. When set on point in a dark, scrappy setting, they provide a fun and unexpected design twist. I designed this block on graph paper and couldn't find a reference to it anywhere, so I named it Churning Star!

FINISHED QUILT
68½" x 85½"

**FINISHED CHURNING
STAR BLOCK**
12" x 12"

Designed and pieced by Jenifer Gaston, quilted by Jill Churchill of Ta Da Quilting Studio

Materials

Yardage is based on 42"-wide fabric.

1 yard of dark-brown print for setting triangles and 1 setting square
⅞ yard of light print for Churn Dash blocks
⅔ yard of medium-brown print for Churn Dash blocks
⅝ yard *each* of 3 dark-brown prints for setting triangles and
    1 setting square
½ yard *each* of 4 dark-brown prints for setting squares
½ yard *each* of 5 light prints for Churning Star blocks
⅓ yard *each* of red, light-blue, dark-blue, gray, and orange prints
    for Churning Star blocks
⅝ yard of brown stripe for binding
5¼ yards of fabric for backing
75" x 92" piece of batting

Cutting

From the ⅞ yard of light print, cut:
4 strips, 3" x 42"; cut into 40 squares, 3" x 3"
5 strips, 1½" x 42"
2 strips, 2½" x 42"; cut into 20 squares, 2½" x 2½"

From the ⅔ yard of medium-brown print, cut:
4 strips, 3" x 42"; cut into 40 squares, 3" x 3"
5 strips, 1½" x 42"

From *each* of the red, light-blue, dark-blue, gray, and orange prints, cut:
2 strips, 3⅞" x 42"; cut into 16 squares, 3⅞" x 3⅞"

From *each* of the ½ yards of light prints, cut:
2 strips, 3½" x 42"; cut into 16 squares, 3½" x 3½"
1 strip, 7¼" x 42"; cut into 4 squares, 7¼" x 7¼"

From the ½ yards of dark-brown prints, cut *a total of*:
10 squares, 12½" x 12½"

From *each* of the ⅝ yards of dark-brown prints, cut:
1 square, 18½" x 18½"; cut into quarters diagonally to make
    4 triangles

Continued on page 67

Make 80 half-square-triangle units with the brown and light prints. Refer to "Chain Piecing" on page 73 for efficient sewing of these units.

Make 80.

2. Sew a light-print 1½" x 42" strip to a medium-brown 1½" x 42" strip. Press the seam allowances toward the brown strip. Make five strip sets. Cut a total of 80 segments, 2½" wide.

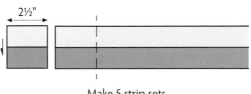

Make 5 strip sets.
Cut 80 segments.

3. Lay out four half-square-triangle units from step 1, four segments from step 2, and one light-print 2½" square as shown. Sew the pieces into rows and press the seam allowances as indicated by the arrows. Sew the rows together to make the Churn Dash block. The block should measure 6½" x 6½". Make 20 blocks.

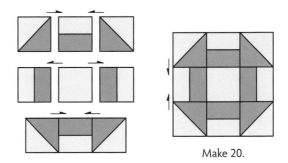

Make 20.

Continued from page 65

From *1* of the dark-brown prints, cut:
1 square, 12½" x 12½"

From the 1 yard of dark-brown print, cut:
1 square, 18½" x 18½"; cut into quarters diagonally to make 4 triangles
2 squares, 9¾" x 9¾"; cut in half diagonally to make 4 triangles
1 square, 12½" x 12½"

From the brown stripe, cut:
8 strips, 2¼" x 42"

Making the Churn Dash Blocks

1. Draw a diagonal line from corner to corner on the wrong side of each light-print 3" square. Layer a marked square right sides together with a medium-brown 3" square and sew ¼" from each side of the drawn line. Cut apart on the line and press seam allowances toward the brown print. Trim and square up to 2½" x 2½".

Making the Churning Star Blocks

1. Referring to "Flying-Geese Units" Method 2 on page 74, make four identical units using four matching red, light-blue, dark-blue, gray, or orange 3⅞" squares and one light 7¼" square.

Make 4.

2. Lay out the four flying-geese units, four matching light-print 3½" squares, and one Churn Dash block as shown. Sew the units into rows and press as indicated. Sew the rows together to make the Churning Star block. It should measure 12½" x 12½".

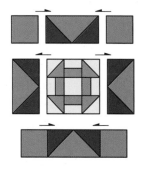 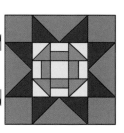

Make 20.

3. Repeat steps 1 and 2 to make 20 blocks.

Assembling the Quilt

1. Referring to the quilt assembly diagram above right, arrange the blocks, setting squares, and setting triangles in diagonal rows. (Note that you'll have two setting triangles left over.) Sew together in rows and press seam allowances toward the setting squares and triangles. Sew the rows together to form the quilt. Press seam allowances in one direction. Add the corner triangles last.

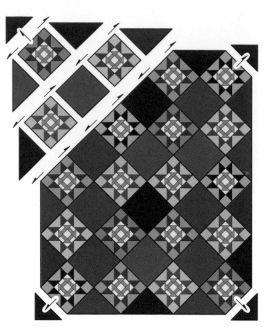

Quilt assembly

2. Trim and square up the sides of the quilt top, leaving a ¼" seam allowance beyond the block points.

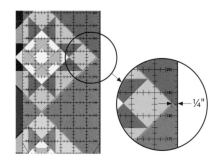

Finishing the Quilt

Refer to "Finishing" on page 77 and "Making a Label" on page 78 for additional information.

1. Layer the quilt top with batting and backing, and baste.

2. Hand or machine quilt as desired. Jill quilted an allover Baptist fan design on my quilt.

3. Trim the excess batting and backing.

4. Prepare and sew the binding to the quilt using the brown stripe 2¼"-wide strips.

5. Add a label to the back, especially if you plan to give the quilt as a gift.

Wool Basics

Most of the projects in this book incorporate wool—from a rug hooked entirely of wool to pieced cotton quilts that feature a bit of wool appliqué. In this section you'll find my tips for both finding wool sources as well as working with wool. It's really quite easy, since wool is a very forgiving fabric.

Gathering and Preparing Wool

For wool appliqué as well as rug hooking, I use 100% wool that has been felted. I use my own hand-dyed wools, but you can find great wool pieces in many quilt and wool shops, and also in thrift stores. If you purchase wool in a quilt or wool shop, check with the salesperson to make sure it's already felted and is colorfast. If you purchase wool items in a thrift shop, follow these steps to prepare the pieces before cutting and sewing.

1. Check all pockets and make sure there isn't anything left in them. I once found a dollar bill in a wonderful herringbone men's suit coat!

2. Wash the items in your washing machine with mild soap, selecting hot wash and cold rinse cycles.

3. Throw the damp wool items in the dryer on high heat. I like to add a dryer sheet, because I like the softness it gives to the wool. This might not be a wise choice, however, if you plan to use fusible web for appliqué, as residue from the fabric softener may prevent the web from sticking to the wool.

4. Remove the wool articles from the dryer and cut out all zippers, buttons, pockets, and linings. I do this after washing and drying so that I'm handling clean wool. In addition, the pieces won't get tangled up during the laundering process as they would if you took them apart beforehand. After washing, the wool also tears more easily, which is helpful when trying to determine the straight of grain and when tearing strips for rug hooking.

A note about yardage. Woven wool, when purchased off the bolt, is usually 54" wide. After felting, it shrinks and will be narrower and shorter by 6" or more. The amount of shrinkage will vary depending on the weave of the wool and how much you felt it. In the materials list for each project, the yardages assume that the wool has been felted and the amounts are enough to make the project shown. If you purchase wool before felting, you will need to purchase more fabric to compensate for shrinkage. You should plan on purchasing about 20% more yardage if the wool has not yet been felted.

Wool Appliqué

Appliquéing with wool is quite simple and easy, as there are no seam allowances to turn under. Here's how I do it.

1. Trace the appliqué patterns onto the dull side of freezer paper. Cut out all shapes about ¼" beyond the drawn line.

Freezer paper

2. Use a dry, hot iron and press the freezer-paper template, shiny side down, onto the appropriate wool color. Cut the piece out on the drawn line and carefully remove the freezer paper.

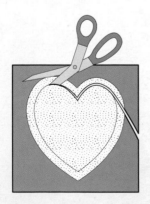

3. Follow any placement guides and position the appliqué pieces onto the background. I like to use tiny appliqué pins or a dab of fabric glue to tack the shapes in place.

4. Stitch the appliqués to the background. My favorite appliqué stitch for wool is just a simple whipstitch. Sometimes I use a running stitch or backstitch. If I'm stitching the outside edge of a wool project, I use a blanket stitch, because it gives a very nice finished look.

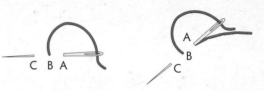

Backstitch

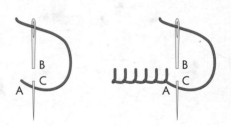

Blanket stitch

Running stitch

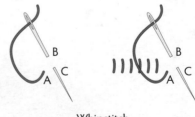

Whipstitch

- For vines and branches, you may want to cut the wool on the bias so that you can curve the strips more easily. If a pattern calls for a vine as narrow as ⅛", you can cut with the grain. Because the strip is so skinny, it will curve just fine without being on the bias, and this will conserve your wool.

- If you have a piece of wool that's loosely woven and prone to fraying, you can make it behave better by either applying fusible web to the wrong side before cutting your appliqués or dabbing the edges with Fray Check before appliquéing.

CHOOSING THREAD

For wool appliqué, I use either wool thread from Aurifil or size 8 hand-dyed pearl cotton thread from Valdani. Valdani offers a collection of hand-dyed pearl cotton with my name on it; these threads are available on my website or in shops (see "Resources" on page 78).

Wool has enough loft to hide your stitches, if that's your goal. If you want the thread to sink into the wool and "disappear," use wool thread in colors to match the appliqué. If you want the thread and stitching to show as an embellishment or accent, a cotton thread such as pearl cotton or floss will stand out. You can also use wool thread in either a complementary or contrasting color, depending on the effect you desire.

EMBROIDERY STITCHES

Embroidery adds special charm to primitive-style wool appliqué. I sometimes combine embroidery stitches with cotton appliqué or use both wool and cotton with embroidery. These are the stitches that I've used in the projects throughout this book.

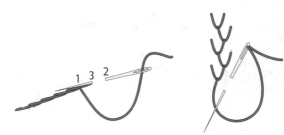

Stem stitch

Feather stitch

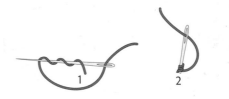

French knot

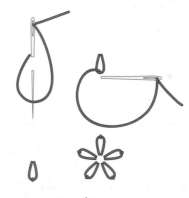

Lazy daisy

Quiltmaking Basics

This is a guide to some of the techniques I've used for the patchwork projects in this book. I've included a few of my favorite tips and guidelines, but there's not space to cover all aspects of quiltmaking. If you need more detailed instructions on specific techniques, you can find free, downloadable information at ShopMartingale.com/HowtoQuilt.

Fabric Selection

When making a primitive-style quilt, I like to use fabrics that play nicely with each other, blend well, and are easy on the eye. I favor blending rather than contrasting fabrics. I tend to shy away from stark whites or bright fabrics, even though color isn't a crucial factor in what makes a project primitive. I love using a variety of small- and medium-scale prints, as well as dots and stripes. Many of my projects are scrappy. I rarely allow any one print to stand out too much, with the exception of a little sparkle or flair that a fun cheddar or pink might add to a scrappy quilt.

I prefer not to prewash my fabric, because I like the way a quilt looks when it crinkles up a bit after washing. Also, by not prewashing, I only have a little pressing to do before cutting. If you purchase good-quality quilting cotton from a quilt shop, you shouldn't need to worry about the fabrics bleeding. If you are concerned about a specific fabric, check it by placing a tiny piece in a bowl with some soap and water for 15 to 20 minutes to see if it runs at all.

Tools

You'll need a few basic tools to make the projects in this book.

Rotary-cutting tools. It's always best to use a new or very sharp blade in your rotary cutter. It makes cutting easier, safer, and more accurate. A cutting mat is essential; the 18" x 24" size will work fine. I also use a 24" x 36" mat, especially when squaring up a quilt. A clear 6" x 12" ruler without too many lines or colors on it is my favorite, but you'll also need a 6" x 24" or 6½" x 24" ruler for cutting strips and trimming the edges of your quilts. For this book, a 6½" square ruler will be handy as well for squaring up units and measuring blocks.

Thread. Cotton thread in 50 to 60 weight is my preference for piecing, because it is very fine and takes up less room in the seams. I also use this thread for machine quilting when I free-motion quilt on my home machine.

Pins. Although I rarely use pins in my piecing, many quilters use them regularly. It's a personal preference. I like to feel with my fingers that things are matching up, and unpinned pieces are easier for me to check at the last minute before the patches go under the needle.

Sandpaper board. Another handy tool for both patchwork and appliqué is a sandpaper board. You can purchase one, or you can buy fine sandpaper and put it on a clipboard. I use this while drawing diagonal lines across the squares when making half-square triangles and flying-geese units. I also like it when tracing around freezer-paper templates for needle-turn appliqué; it keeps the fabric from slipping around.

Marking tools. Some of my go-to marking tools are mechanical pencils, chalk wheels, and chalk pencils. The chalk wheels are great for marking quilting lines as well as for drawing on wool. I really like the Sewline fabric pencils, especially the Sewline Trio Colors mechanical pencil that has black, white, and pink lead.

Seam ripper. The usefulness of this tool goes without saying, but I'll go ahead and say it anyway! I believe everyone needs a seam ripper once in a while, and I definitely like to keep mine handy. I measure each block as it comes off the machine to catch any mistakes immediately. I can fix the block right away, figure out what went wrong, and keep it from happening to the rest of the blocks so I don't have a pile of them to correct at the end!

Patchwork

Before you start any project, I suggest reading through the instructions carefully. I do this to make sure that I know the order of things, and if there is a technique I don't understand, I can look it up and practice it before I begin. When piecing all of the projects in this book, use a ¼" seam allowance unless the instructions state otherwise.

PRESSING

When I am ready to cut my fabric, I like to steam press it and then use a fabric starch, such as Best Press, especially on wovens. This makes the cutting nice, neat, and precise, and the fabric is less likely to stretch out of shape.

Before piecing, I turn off the steam on my iron. I use high heat without steam for cotton. I feel that using steam while piecing can cause some fabric patches to shrink, therefore making the blocks come out the wrong size and preventing them from fitting together nicely. When pressing seam allowances I hold the iron in place firmly, lifting and pressing rather than moving the iron around.

CHAIN PIECING

In a couple of the projects you will be making multiple half-square-triangle units. This is a good time to do chain piecing. Just draw the lines, pair up the squares, and feed them through your machine one right after the other. When you get to the end, spin the last one around, and head down the other side of the drawn lines one right after the other again.

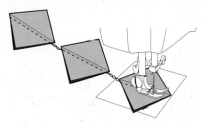

Clip all the threads after chain piecing, cut on all the drawn lines, and then press with a hot, dry iron. Press all seam allowances toward the darker fabric, which will help the seams nest together at intersections when being matched up with other patchwork later.

MAKING STRIP SETS

When sewing strips together to make strip sets, press each seam after it is sewn to keep it from becoming curved. Use a hot, dry iron and press, using a lifting-and-pressing motion rather than moving the iron around, so that the strip doesn't get pulled out of shape. Press toward the darker fabric whenever possible. When cutting across strip sets, align the ruler lines with the seam line and raw edges of the strip set to make sure everything is nice and square as you cut the segments.

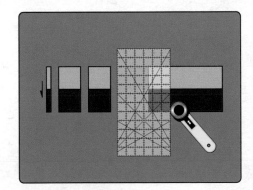

FLYING-GEESE UNITS

I use two methods of making flying geese. Method 1 makes one unit at a time. Method 2 yields four units.

Method 1. For this method you'll cut a rectangle and two squares.

1. Draw a diagonal line from corner to corner on the wrong side of each square.

2. Place a marked square on one end of the rectangle. Sew on the line. Cut away just the outside part of the square, leaving a ¼" seam allowance and keeping the rectangle corner intact. Press the inside triangle toward the corner.

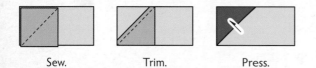

Sew.   Trim.   Press.

3. Place the second square on the other end of the rectangle, making sure the diagonal line is going in the correct direction. Sew, trim, and press as before.

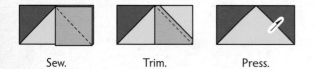

Sew.   Trim.   Press.

By leaving the rectangle intact, you always have that perfectly cut rectangle to use as a guide if the triangles aren't perfect after they are pressed toward the corner. When you line up the unit to sew it to other pieces, you can follow the rectangle for a perfect outcome! This is a trick my mother taught me.

Method 2. For this method, you'll cut a large square and four small squares to make four identical flying-geese units.

1. Draw a diagonal line from corner to corner on the wrong side of the four small squares.

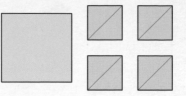

2. Place two of the marked squares right sides together on the large square. They should be diagonal from each other with the points in the center overlapping a little. Sew ¼" from the line on both sides. Cut on the line, and press the seam allowances toward the darker fabric.

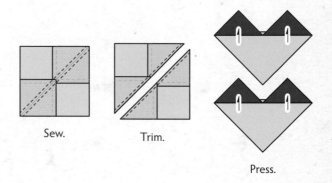

Sew.   Trim.

Press.

3. Place a marked square right sides together on each of the units from step 2, aligning the raw edges as shown. Sew ¼" from the line on both sides. Cut apart on the line and press the seam allowances toward the darker fabrics. You'll have four identical flying geese!

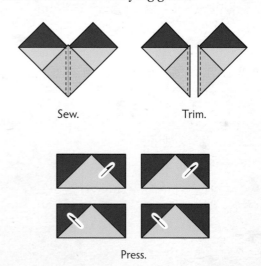

Sew.   Trim.

Press.

Needle-Turn Appliqué

After many years of trying numerous appliqué methods, I have found that I like needle-turn appliqué the best when working with cotton fabrics. It involves minimal preparation, so you can get right to the fun part of stitching! All you need are freezer paper, a fabric marker, scissors, pins, needle, and thread.

For needle-turn appliqué I use size 11 milliner's needles. They are long, thin, and flexible. You can get them with a large eye, but I still sometimes need that trusty needle threader! I generally use tiny appliqué pins to secure my pieces to the background while sewing, although sometimes I use a little bit of fabric glue instead of pins. I prefer a fine thread, such as 100-weight silk or 60-weight polyester or cotton, for stitching. A fine thread in a color that matches the appliqué will blend in and hardly show up at all.

Follow these steps for needle-turn appliqué, or use your own preferred method. If you are using a fusible-web product, you will need to reverse the patterns and follow the instructions that come with the fusible product.

1. Trace the pattern for the design onto the dull side of freezer paper and cut out the template on the drawn line.

2. Press the freezer paper onto the right side of the appliqué fabric, and trace around the template with a marking tool that disappears or can be easily erased. I use a sandpaper board (page 72) underneath the fabric when tracing, but it's not essential.

3. Cut the shape from the fabric, adding a ¼" seam allowance outside the drawn line.

4. Remove the paper and fasten the appliqué piece on the background fabric with a pin or a little fabric glue.

5. Thread a needle and knot the end of the thread. Bring the needle up from the wrong side of the appliqué piece through the drawn line. This will result in a knot that is hidden in the folded edge of the appliqué.

6. Fold under the seam allowance where you will take the first few stitches, creasing it along the drawn line. Hold the folded-under section with the thumb and forefinger of your non-sewing hand. Take the needle down into the background right next to where the thread emerges from the fold. Bring the needle back up about ⅛" away and catch just a thread or two at the fold of the appliqué. Go back down through the background, hiding your stitch almost under the appliqué fold. Repeat, bringing the needle back up again ⅛" away. Continue making this blind stitch. As you move along your appliqué piece, tuck the seam allowance under with your needle, holding it with your non-sewing hand. Turn under just enough for a few stitches at a time, and you will get into a rhythm.

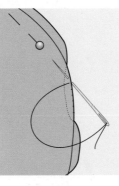

For tight inside curves or points, make a little clip into the seam allowance, but don't clip until you are almost there, to keep the raw edge from fraying.

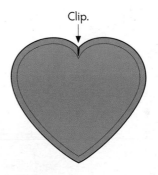

Clip.

For outside points, stitch to the point, make an extra stitch, pull the seam allowance on the other side of the point back, and trim to reduce the bulk. Then sweep the seam allowance down and under to continue stitching the next side.

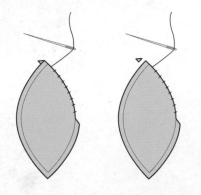

Making Bias Stems and Vines

Cutting strips on the bias allows you to make smoothly curved flower stems and flowing vines. I use a bias-tape maker, but you can make them without one as well. The bias strips for projects are all cut at ⅞" wide and will result in vines with a finished width of ⅜". You'll need a ⅜" bias-tape maker, available at most quilt shops and online. When pressing, use steam and a hot iron. A spritz of spray sizing or starch as you press will add body and maintain crisp edges.

1. Cut the required number of strips on the bias, as indicated in the project instructions.

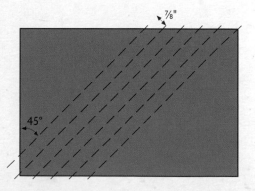

2. Piece the strips if necessary by placing them right sides together at a 90° angle, aligning the raw edges and offsetting them to sew using a ¼" seam allowance. Sew together and press the seam allowances open.

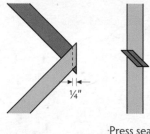

Press seam allowances open.

3. Insert the strip into the bias-tape maker and pin one end of the strip to your ironing surface. Pull the bias-tape maker along the strip and press.

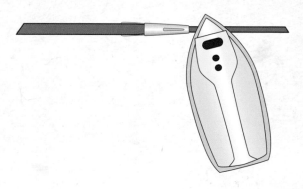

To make vines without the bias-tape maker, simply fold the raw edges of the strip inward ¼" and press. Your strips are ready to appliqué.

Finishing

After completing your quilt top, prepare it for quilting by giving it a final pressing, making sure seam allowances are pressed flat without pleats on either side. Trim any long threads so that they won't show through the quilt top. If you need additional details on any of the following steps, refer to ShopMartingale.com/HowtoQuilt for free illustrated information.

1. Piece the backing fabric if needed, and trim so that it's 6" larger than the quilt top. If you'll be sending your quilt to a professional machine quilter, check with the quilter regarding the size of the backing and batting.

2. Layer the quilt with the backing and batting and baste with safety pins, thread, or a basting spray. I like to use basting spray—it's quick and easy. When using the spray, you'll need to wash the quilt after it's quilted and bound. This removes the spray and gives the quilt a crinkled, antique look that I like.

3. Quilt as desired by hand or machine. See "Primitive-Style Quilting," right, for ideas.

4. Trim the excess batting and backing; square up the corners of the quilt top as needed. Use your longest ruler for the sides and a square ruler for the corners.

5. Piece the binding strips together end to end to make one long strip. Press in half lengthwise with wrong sides together. Sew the binding to the quilt.

The Finishing Touch

I love to use a striped fabric for binding—it's such a fun and interesting look. Many of my quilts have a binding from the same fabric as the border; I do that when I don't want to draw attention to the binding. But as I was designing the quilts for this book and choosing fabric, I found that stripes made sweet frames to complete the quilts.

Primitive-Style Quilting

To give your quilt a primitive look, use an old-fashioned quilting pattern, such as a Baptist fan, shown above, or choose a grid design. For hand quilting, big-stitch quilting with size 8 pearl cotton does the trick and immediately reads as primitive.

If you prefer to machine quilt, and I do this often, I stitch a fairly small-scale stipple design. Then when the quilt is washed, it will have that wonderful crinkled look that antique quilts have.

If your quilt includes appliqué, outline around the motifs first. Then either stipple, echo quilt, or hand quilt a grid that stops at the outline of the motif, picking back up on the other side. If the appliqué motifs are large, add a little quilting on the motif as well. You might quilt around the center circle of a flower or quilt some wavy lines on a watering can.

In general, keep the quilting simple and unfussy. You don't want it to detract from the quilt itself.

Making a Label

I always enjoy adding a label to the back of my projects. It can be simple, giving just a date and your name. Here's how I label most of my quilts and hooked rugs.

1. Cut a rectangle or square of muslin, about ½" larger than the desired finished size.

2. Iron a piece of freezer paper to the wrong side of the fabric.

3. Use Pigma Micron pens or other permanent fabric markers in different colors to draw a little design on the fabric, such as one of the appliqué shapes used on the front of the quilt. Color in the shape and then add your name, date, and the town where you live.

4. Remove the paper backing and press the seam allowance to the back. Pin in place on the back of the project and blind stitch around the edges.

You can also use rubber stamps and fabric ink, or create an image on your computer and print it onto a cotton sheet designed specifically for printers.

Resources

LONG-ARM QUILTING

Ta Da Quilting Studio
Jill Churchill
814-520-5774
tadaquilting.blogspot.com

Bolts and Quarters Quilt Shop
Brian D. McCoy
304-428-4933
boltsandquartersquiltshop.com

Sew Graceful Quilting
Darleen Szabo
479-372-7403
sewgracefulquilting.com

HAND-DYED WOOL, KITS, AND VALDANI HAND-DYED PEARL COTTON

www.woolenwillowdesigns.com
jenifromthewillow.blogspot.com

AURIFIL WOOL THREAD

Primitivequiltsandprojects.com

Acknowledgments

I thank God for the blessings of a wonderful family, full of love, support, and encouragement; for my husband, Glen, who has supported me in all my creative and business endeavors and didn't mind the sewing supplies and wool all over the tables while I was working on this book, and for my kids, Kristen and Kristopher, who are wonderful and creative themselves, and who have given me so much joy being their mother.

I want to thank my parents, George and Mary Falcsik, for their unending support, love, and encouragement. They instilled in me a love of making things with what we had on hand as a kid. In addition, they have always been there for my sister and me to help with the shop in any way that was needed.

And I thank my sister, Gretchen Smith, for all the years in business together and for editing all my patterns and making them look pretty. I know that wasn't an easy job with all my run-on sentences! We had a wonderful shop that was a dream come true for us.

I also want to thank the entire team at Martingale for making this dream of a book come true for me—and for encouraging me to do it!

To my awesome friends Carolyn, Janice, Vicki, and Sandy: thank you for helping me get these projects finished. Your sewing and stitching is wonderful! And cousin Jill Churchill, Brian McCoy, and Darlene Szabo for quilting some of my quilts, lightning fast, and so beautifully!

Meet the Author

Jenifer Gaston, or Jeni as everyone calls her, has been sewing and crafting with her three sisters since she was a little girl. Her mother was always sewing, knitting, crocheting, or making clothes for the girls of the family. Jeni's two older sisters sang and performed with their guitars in weddings and plays, so they often needed gowns. You can imagine the pretty fabrics in their mother's scrap bag. Jeni and her sisters loved using those scraps for doll dresses; they had the best-dressed Skippers and Barbies in town!

Jeni started quilting about 21 years ago, when her youngest child was a toddler. A few years later, she fell in love with wool. She began dying wool, designing rug-hooking patterns, and teaching others how to hook rugs. Her younger sister, Gretchen, joined her in these endeavors, and in 1999 they started an online business called the Rug Hooking Store. Gretchen lived in Texas, and Jeni was in West Virginia. They dreamed of having a shop together, so in 2004 Gretchen moved her family home, and they opened the Woolen Willow Quilt Shop. The sisters held many classes and great events as they ran the shop for 10 wonderful years, with their father and mother lending a hand whenever and wherever needed. Woolen Willow was a top shop featured in the 2007 issue of *Quilt Sampler*.

In 2011, Jeni and Gretchen, along with a third sister, Judy, began publishing *Primitive Quilts and Projects* magazine. Although the quilt shop has since closed, the fourth sister, Sally, has started organizing quilting and rug-hooking retreats, drawing people from all over the country.

While the purpose of this section is to tell you a bit about the author, Jeni readily acknowledges that she wouldn't be who she is without her wonderful family.